BOOMERS
ON THE EDGE

Also by Terry D. Hargrave

Loving Your Parents When They Can No Longer Love You

Strength and Courage for Caregivers

BOOMERS
ON THE EDGE

Three Realities That Will Change Your Life Forever

TERRY HARGRAVE

ZONDERVAN®

ZONDERVAN.com/
AUTHORTRACKER
follow your favorite authors

 ZONDERVAN®

Boomers on the Edge

Copyright © 2008 by Terry Hargrave

Requests for information should be addressed to:

Zondervan, *Grand Rapids, Michigan 49530*

Library of Congress Cataloging-in-Publication Data

Hargrave, Terry D.
    Boomers on the edge : three realities that will change your life forever /
    Terry D. Hargrave.
        p.   cm.
      ISBN 978-0-310-27659-3 (softcover)
       1. Baby boom generation—Religious life. 2. Intergenerational relations—
Religious aspects—Christianity. I. Title.
    BV4579.5H365   2007
    248.8'5—dc22   2007049132

All Scripture quotations, unless otherwise indicated, are taken from the *Holy Bible: New International Version*®. NIV®. Copyright © 1973, 1978, 1984 by International Bible Society. Used by permission of Zondervan. All rights reserved.

Interior design by Beth Shagene

Printed in the United States of America

08 09 10 11 12 13 • 23 22 21 20 19 18 17 16 15 14 13 12 11 10 9 8 7 6 5 4 3 2 1

"We do not lose heart.
Though outwardly we are wasting away,
yet inwardly we are being renewed day by day."
2 Corinthians 4:16

CONTENTS

INTRODUCTION: FROM THE CORNER TO THE EDGE

We are a generation that feels things deeply. Just think of how many thousands of us marched on high school, college, and university campuses, protesting for civil rights or against the war in Vietnam.

We are a generation unafraid of new things. Whether it is the innovative music of the Beatles revamping rock and roll or the embracing of computerization to the point where a digital world becomes a way of life, we move and change whenever things look exciting or promising.

We are a generation that is committed. Very few generations have made the effort to understand, nurture, and provide as many opportunities for their children as we have. We try to ensure that our offspring have healthy self-esteems and therefore every chance to succeed.

We feel things deeply; we are unafraid of challenges; we are committed. Our generation, the "baby boomers," has remade society by our sheer numbers, new attitudes, and distinctive behavior. But even with all our unique attributes – and as much as we have changed society – no one has ever called us "the Greatest Generation."

To the generation that experienced the hardship of the Great Depression in the 1930s, the horror of World War II in the '40s, and the fear and paranoia of the Cold War in the '50s, we have often appeared selfish, self-absorbed, and irresponsible. It has seemed to them (and perhaps to much of the world and maybe even to ourselves) that we have never had our character tested in the crucible. It has almost been as though our experiences in reshaping attitudes toward civil rights and government, embracing the hard realities of computerization and the changes it has prompted in the world of employment, and facing the challenges of educating our children in an often dangerous atmosphere have not mattered in the eyes of the previous generation.

Perhaps no one has much noticed, but the boomer generation has demonstrated great commitment, resiliency, and grit in the past fifty years, all while remaining reasonably well connected emotionally. Maybe it is little noticed, but the boomers have what is commonly referred to as "heart."

And it is a good thing that we have heart! Frankly, we are going to need it.

Here we are, in our fifties and sixties, perhaps thinking we were just about finished with making an impact on the world – when God taps us lightly on the shoulder, as if to say, "Ah, but there is one more thing."

God has chosen *us* to embark on the greatest sociological change of this century, the most profound since we changed the face of history when we burst onto the world scene in the years following World War II. Yes, we are the generation of the baby boomers, and just as we changed education, social mores, and the American Dream in the last century, so we will change how life and family are "done" in this one. If previous generations have doubted our grit to stand in the crucible, we are getting ready to be tested as we face three decades that promise to be every bit as challenging as the eras of the Great Depression, World War II, and the Cold War.

God has used generations in the past to make their marks and fight through economic depressions, win wars, evangelize remote parts of the world, set up governments, and abolish slavery. With everything that we boomers already have changed, it will be our task yet again to make our mark and once more change the world. This comes at a time when we may have thought we would be slowing down—but the reality is that we are on the very edge of a totally different way of living.

So here they are—the three simple realities that will change our lives and the lives of our children forever:

- caring for aging parents
- raising an adult child who has moved back home
- retiring from a career, only to find that we must return to work

These three sociological factors—which, by the way, God has been molding and shaping for the past half century through medicine, economics, and lifestyle—will thrust us boomers right back into the vortex of change. These factors have been at work for many years and are now backing us into the corner. Many of us have seen these things edging in on us, but the thought of dealing with so many unknowns has felt overwhelming, given the press of so many current responsibilities. To preserve our sanity, we have tried to ignore these realities and just "not think about it." But the reality of parents who are aging, adult children who are moving back home, and our own lack of financial means to retire and maintain our lifestyle for possibly twenty to thirty remaining years, has not relented.

With the advent of a new century, we are no longer cornered, but we have been forced to open the window and perch ourselves on the precarious edge of acknowledgment. No matter how hard the task or difficult the adjustment, the pressure of living on this edge has forced us to look these factors straight in the eye and take responsibility for the changes and challenges that now face our families.

Will others question whether we are up to this task? Perhaps. But I do not. I believe that we boomers are poised to make the dramatic sacrifices necessary and adjust to new responsibilities that will rightly place *us* as one of the great generations, worthy of song and story. We are set to become the first Caregiving Generation. I believe we have been commissioned for this task. It is our time! So let's look at the facts of what we face.

REALITY 1: Caring for Aging Parents

Bob and Sue are great people who have great plans for their retirement. Bob worked as a mechanical engineer, and Sue taught in the public schools after staying home for the first few years with their two children. Now, with both children married and three young grandchildren, Bob and Sue felt they had arrived at the edge of recreational travel, planning long stays with their children who lived in different states and being able to have a large and positive effect on their grandchildren. They had reached the age of sixty-two with plenty of retirement resources, and nothing seemed surer than the life they had plotted out. It all seemed as reliable as one of Bob's mechanical drawings.

That is, until the last year. In those few months, the direction of Bob and Sue's retirement life shifted significantly. Sue's parents, ages eighty-four and eighty-five, were the first to show problems. Her mother fell and broke her hip, and after the surgery and a short convalescence at a nursing facility, Sue convinced herself that her mother could return home, with some help and care from her father. But it quickly became clear that Sue's father hadn't been doing well for some time. It wasn't that he wasn't willing to care for his wife. He was! But his memory, energy level, and dexterity had been waning for many years — without Sue noticing. The truth? Sue's mother had been giving increasingly substantial care to her father for a long time, and he simply lacked the capability to care for her. With Sue's mother in need of significant care, Sue found, to her surprise, that she had *two* parents who needed two to three hours of her time each day to get their meals, get to doctor appointments, and make sure they took their medications.

But that wasn't the end of the story. Bob's father had died when Bob was in his early fifties. Since then, Bob's mother had always functioned well on her own, with minimal help from Bob and Sue — primarily just a bit of help managing some long-term finances. But within the last year, Bob started receiving overdue notices on bills from the electric and telephone companies. When Bob arranged to have his mother's bills paid directly out of the account, he thought he had solved the problem — until he received a call from the bank, informing him that his mother's account was overdrawn. And it was not overdrawn by a little, but by $1,500!

Although his mother could not remember the incident, Bob discovered that she had written a check for several thousand dollars to a scam artist who guaranteed a miraculous return on her money.

Unfortunately, the problems were not confined to erratic financial behavior. Bob's mother also started calling him at strange hours during the night, asking questions about where things were located in her house. She frequently lost items such as her car keys and purse. And he soon began to notice the small things that indicated she wasn't taking care of herself like she always had. Her hair often seemed a little askew, and she stopped wearing the small amount of makeup she had always worn to cover age spots. A distinct odor indicated that she was no longer regularly bathing or brushing her teeth.

After taking his mother for a visit to the doctor, Bob heard the words he dreaded. "We'll run some tests," the physician said, "but I think you need to be realistic about what's happening here. I suspect your mother is in the early stages of Alzheimer's disease."

Like most boomers, Bob and Sue assumed they would retire in much the same way that their parents had retired. Instead, they got a big surprise: they will be spending their early retirement years managing and caring for aging parents.

Most of us have heard that the boomer generation will significantly change the face of aging in America as its members reach retirement age. And this is undeniably true. Between 2010 and 2029, some 76 million boomers will reach the age of sixty-five. But by age sixty-five, seventy, and even seventy-five, most boomers will likely still be healthy, active, and vital. In other words, it won't *feel* as though we will have become part of the aging population.

The group that will first change the meanings and definitions of aging will be our parents, as they now live longer than any previous generation. Where most of our parents' grandparents died in their sixties and seventies, our grandparents died mostly in their seventies or eighties. More and more, however, our parents will live into their late eighties or nineties. So do the math! If our parents are living and needing care in their late eighties, most of us will likely be in our late fifties or sixties. And that's when the job of caregiving will fall to us. What we thought was going to be a retirement party and a "slowing down" time is actually going to be a time of ratcheting up to face the challenges of being the first Caregiving Generation.

And we will not be the first Caregiving Generation simply

because other generations never gave care to their aged parents and grandparents. They certainly did in faithful and effective ways. But we *will* be the first generation who gives care *en masse*, as almost every family will spend at least some time caring for an older parent. We also will be the first who will give care over a distinctly longer period of time, perhaps as many as ten years. Previous generations have cared for elders, but none had so many elders to care for, and none for as long.

So why are things different? What has happened to significantly change the face of aging for the oldest of the old? Simply put, advances in medical science. Medicine in the last century has made enormous strides in fighting the effects of disease and injury. At the turn of the twentieth century, average longevity in the United States was a little over forty-seven years; the number one cause of death was influenza. But as the causes and care for diseases became better understood, average longevity lengthened through the decades until today a male's life expectancy is almost seventy-six years, while a female can expect to live to be just over age eighty. Think of what that means. In one hundred years, average longevity has increased *more than thirty years*. Quite a remarkable achievement for medical science!

And the result is a mushrooming number of people who will live far into their eighties, with a significant percentage living to be age ninety and above. Most of us boomers will reach age sixty with at least one parent living. Simply put, there will be more older people around than ever before, and not just because of us boomers entering the aging ranks. Our parents will be living much longer, and therefore won't be leaving the group of the aging until much later.

Just because medical science has so successfully battled diseases and other problems that cause death, however, does not mean that it has eradicated problems that cause ill health. For instance, think of an elderly person with heart disease. Many people in their late seventies or early eighties have heart bypass operations these days. Most often, these operations are "successful" in that the person's life is extended for years, with issues that are manageable. But is the person returned to pristine health? Probably not. Most likely, the person will recover somewhat but will have to struggle with a variety of chronic problems that, twenty years earlier, would have killed him or her.

In this way, modern medicine has made great strides in converting *terminal* disease into *chronic* disease. In other words, our grandparents usually died of the problems that now can be managed medically for five, ten, or even fifteen years. When I was a boy, some older people in my extended family lived into their seventies and eighties. But when they became ill with pneumonia, cancer, or heart disease, or even if they broke a hip or suffered a bad fall, they were much more likely to die in a matter of months. With the medical interventions available today, however, an elder may fall prey to these same problems and yet expect to live for several more years.

Two factors, more than any others, will force boomers to change the face of aging and so become the first Caregiving Generation: (1) Almost all of us will have at least one parent who lives well into his or her eighties, where health is most likely to decline and care is required, and (2) most of our parents who need care will live for five or ten years *after* they begin to need our care, instead of those of previous generations who lived perhaps months or a year or two. We are the first because almost all of us will face the job of caregiving – and we will be giving that care for a significant portion of our lives.

Like Bob and Sue, who thought they were in for a life of retirement, travel, and enjoyment of children and grandchildren, we will likely find the decade of our sixties strewn with struggles about how to make sense of our parents' finances, ease their transition toward depending on us, and negotiate the pitfalls of doctor appointments, housing, nutrition, medication, and supervision. It will do more than get in the way of the plans we make for ourselves; it will totally change the way we live and the direction of our financial, social, and emotional goals. *Nothing* in this century will change family life more than the fact that we will be required to care for aging family members for a good portion of our lives.

REALITY 2: **Raising Adult Children Returning Home**

Karen and Joe were working hard to try to give their children the college education that their own parents had not been able to provide. Joe, an electrician, took extra jobs on weekends to pay for college tuition, and Karen worked a retail job on the weekends in addition to her regular warehouse job. Their hard work paid off, as all three children entered college within six years of each other.

Their oldest son did well in college, got his education degree, and went on to begin a teaching and coaching career in a local high school. Their next oldest attended college for two years and then met "the man of her dreams," a fellow her brother's age who also worked as a teacher and coach. The daughter dropped out of college to marry this man, but Karen and Joe were quite sure she'd eventually finish her education after she had a few children. Their youngest child—perhaps the most talented—went to college on a partial music scholarship. Although his talents impressed everyone in the community, he did not seem to have any solid career plans after college graduation.

With no plans or prospects, Karen and Joe's youngest son moved back home. To them, it felt like a flashback to an earlier time. Their son settled into his old room and took up many of the habits and behaviors he had had in high school, acting as if his college education had never taken place. When they inquired about his plans, he became defensive and angry. "You don't know how bad it makes me feel that I have to live at home," he declared. "I'm looking for a job, and I'll get out of your hair as soon as I can find a good enough job to afford to move out." They loved their twenty-three-year-old son very much and did not want to make him angry or feel bad, but to Karen and Joe, their son seemed to lack motivation, almost to the point of laziness. Certainly, he didn't seem eager to find a job.

The fact that Karen and Joe had an adult son living at home without much in the way of job prospects caused enough stress, but then a new shock hit the family. Their twenty-seven-year-old daughter showed up at their house one day with her four- and two-year-old children—not just for a visit, but to stay. She informed her parents that her husband of seven years had had an affair, and she was going to divorce him. Karen and Joe did their best to understand the situation and discuss the possibilities for reconciliation, but their daughter insisted, "We've been drifting apart for years, and I've come to the conclusion that nothing will ever change. I've tried to make it with him, but now I'm through." Devastated and confused, their daughter dragged herself to her old room, made a pallet for the four-year-old, and lay down in her old bed, her two-year-old close beside her.

Karen and Joe crawled into bed that night wondering how all this change could have overtaken them so quickly. Only a few months before, they had been empty nesters looking forward to the happy prospect of quitting their extra jobs and slowing down their lives. Suddenly they had two of their adult children sleeping in their old rooms, with two small grandchildren besides. In just a few days, they had gone from a household of two to a household of six.

The phenomenon of adult children moving back home is new, and it's growing. The odds of an unmarried twenty-six-year-old living at home in 1970 were about 1 in 10. Today, the likelihood of a twenty-six-year-old living at home is about 1 in 5. If we take into account the number of adult children who move back home for a significant period of time after the traditional college age of twenty-two, the number is almost 40 percent.

This same trend is true when it comes to parents' raising their children's children. In 1980, only about three million children (or 4 percent of all children) were being raised by grandparents. Over 60 percent of the time, these grandparents also had their children (their grandchildren's parent) in the house as well. Today, the number of children being raised by grandparents is 8 million, or perhaps as high as 10 percent of all children. But as opposed to twenty-five years ago, only about one-fourth of the grandchildren's parents are also present in the household. More than 2.5 million grandparents have the responsibility of raising their grandchildren – and chances are as high as 1 in 3 that children will eventually spend at least some of their growing-up years in the homes of their grandparents.

Call them what you will – "kidults," "boomerang kids," or "twixters" – but what we have is a distinct trend of adult children moving back home instead of living on their own. It is easy to blame this phenomenon on irresponsible and uncommitted kids, but the truth is a bit more complicated. No doubt some adult kids are just plain lazy, but three issues help to explain why so many adult children are moving back home.

The primary reason is the significant economic shift over the last fifty years, which has made it more difficult to establish oneself. The chief issue that makes the economy different is *the amount of debt* that adult kids carry. With the unprecedented rise in college tuition costs, student loans are almost a given. Over the last decade, student loans have increased by almost 85 percent. More than two-thirds of students who owe money for their education owe more than $10,000 – and this is debt carried only for education; it doesn't include car loans or credit card debt. Like the culture at large, the amount of debt accumulated by young adults makes saving virtually impossible and the ability to meet household expenses uncertain. Simply stated, the debt accumulated by young adult children in their first years as adults seriously impairs their ability to become independent.

The second issue is *earning power*. Even thirty years ago, a college degree was virtually an ironclad guarantee of employment. Since 1970, however, the number of people who attend college has increased by almost 53 percent. As the general population becomes more educated, typically the value of a college degree drops. Annual earnings among men aged twenty-five to thirty-four dropped more than 17 percent over the last thirty years. Even among males with only high school diplomas, the average earning power dropped more than 12 percent in thirty years. Combine this with the steady rate of inflation over the last twenty years, and it's easy to see why many young adults simply can't afford to establish their independence.

The final issue is *housing*. Fifty years ago, a person could plan on spending about 27 percent of his or her income to secure housing. Today, that number is likely to be about 45 percent. But even that doesn't tell the whole story. Fifty years ago, people had many more stable, relatively crime-free, middle class housing options. What used to be lower middle class housing has evolved into lower income housing, to a large extent making "cheap rent" almost unheard-of.

These three factors have conspired to produce adult children who have significant debt, limited earning power, and the inability to afford a place of their own. The solution to this economic challenge is clear: the young people move back home.

It is likely that half of us boomers will welcome our adult children back into our homes for a significant period of time. But the above-mentioned issues aren't the only reasons our adult kids return home. Sadly, many of our adult kids are not very good at relationships.

Remember Karen and Joe, whose daughter moved back home after leaving her husband? Many of us rightly see the divorce rate as a significant contributor in adult children moving back home. Statistics show that almost 9 percent of marriages will end within two years of the wedding – the good news is that the divorce rate has actually declined a bit from the 1980s. Still, divorce remains one of the primary reasons that adult children move back home. After a divorce, it is typically the female adult child who moves back home with her children in tow. Without the financial means to care for herself and her children, she often seeks the support necessary not only for housing but also for retraining to get a job that pays enough to support herself. This process usually involves the daughter going back to college (or getting vocational training), while her parents are left to foot the financial bill and provide care for the children.

While there is no doubt that the divorce rate contributes to the number of adult children moving back home, the real relational culprit is the fact that many adult children simply do not marry. First-time marriages have declined 50 percent since 1970, while the cohabitation rate has increased tenfold to 4.2 million couples. Cohabitation relationships are twice as likely to break up as marriages, and 29 percent of them break up within two years. Thirty years ago, only about 15 percent of cohabitating couples had children; today, almost 40 percent of cohabitation breakups involve children. These adult kids move back home with their parents to seek the relational and financial support to "recover" from their relationship mistakes.

While adult children move back home for other reasons as well, most often the primary reason is related to either finances or relational failures, or both. And once adult children return home, it's not so easy to figure out how to get them out on their own.

Again, we boomers are a pioneering generation with regard to this phenomenon — and we have very little guidance about how to be helpful and yet teach boundaries and responsibility. We did plenty of reading about how to raise our children when they were young, but where is the "rulebook" on raising *adult* children? The reality is that most of our adult children are not lazy or uncommitted; they are simply running into the hardness of what life offers in this day and age. We love them and simply cannot fathom turning them away.

What are we boomer parents to do? We must move into this challenge to find a specific way of finishing the parenting job, something that hasn't been necessary before. The task involves a new and collaborative effort of raising healthy adult children in the face of a changing world with new challenges. It is all about helping our adult children to grow up.

REALITY 3: Retiring Only to Go Back to Work

Things for Rob and Cindy looked much more secure twenty years ago than they do today. They were in their mid-forties and both working in the airline industry, she as a flight attendant and he as an aircraft mechanic. But slowly and surely, the erratic business health of their industry chipped away at their secure jobs and made them feel always on the edge of unemployment.

First, contract disputes resulted in a substantial reduction in wages and benefits. Then Rob's airline filed for bankruptcy protection. Although the airline restructured and finally emerged from bankruptcy, the additional concessions required from almost all company workers left a definite financial gap for Rob and Cindy and affected their financial confidence. They struggled but managed to string together enough money to keep their family of four afloat. Having survived their industry's tumultuous years and managing to stay employed, at ages sixty-two and sixty, they began looking at their prospects for retirement. They expected to be able to retire in a couple of years, without the stress and headache of wondering if they would have paychecks.

They discovered, of course, a much more sobering reality.

They found that all of those concessions and restructurings over the years had had a significantly negative effect on their pensions. Concessions had translated into a far lower level of funding for the pension programs. When Rob's airline restructured, the company defaulted on its employee pension plan. Although the government took over the defaulted pension, the result was a greatly reduced pension benefit. When they started running the hard numbers, Rob and Cindy found that their pension benefit would amount to only about 40 percent of what they had expected only fifteen years earlier. At the time of all of the concessions and restructurings, they had reasoned that they had to "give in" in order to keep their jobs. Perhaps that was true; but the effect of their relenting *then* was proving to have a huge effect on their retirement prospects *now*. Rob has started training as a truck driver, and he and Cindy plan to spend the first five to ten years of their "retirement" working. They reason that at least they'll feel much less pressure, and they'll be able to be together as they make long hauls across the country.

Rob and Cindy are not alone. About a full third of boomers will find themselves in similar situations. Several factors have conspired and several threats loom, all of which point toward reduced income and retirement resources for boomers.

The first issue is the one facing Rob and Cindy. Many traditional companies, agencies, and organizations have found it impossible to fund their pension programs at the rates necessary to pay promised benefits to employees. If you have a pension program and you are under the impression that a pool of money is waiting for you in an account somewhere, please know that you are sadly mistaken. Pensions depend on good growth in investment returns, impeccable management, and, most important, adequate funding from employment sources. But many pension programs have not been properly managed. As more benefits have come due, less and less funding has been available. The result? More than twenty companies have defaulted on their pension plans in the past three years. The Pension Benefit Guarantee Corporation (PBGC), a federal pension insurance program, will pick up some of the slack, but with so many companies defaulting, the program's financial ability to pay is in doubt. Most likely, surviving pensions will pay much lower benefits than employees expected. If the pension defaults to the PBGC, the employee will likely receive only dimes on the dollar of the benefits owed. And how will they make up for the gap between what they expected to receive and what they will actually get?

Like Rob and Cindy, they will probably have to find work.

Most companies and agencies have recognized this problem and have started moving toward defined contribution plans or cash balance plans. In these types of plans, the employer offers to match, up to a certain percentage, an employee contribution to a 401(k) or similar retirement account. In most cases, the account belongs to the employee after an initial period of vesting, and so a person is "guaranteed" the money in the account.

While these plans boast some advantages, such as greater control by the individual and more portability after a job change, they also involve huge problems that are likely to result in insufficient resources for retirement. First, there is the challenge of savings. Savings in the United States have declined to the lowest level ever. We have a voracious appetite for "things," and while consumer debt is at an all-time high, we do not save enough for virtually anything. This is also true for retirement. What does it matter if a company will match an employee contribution if the employee doesn't make substantial contributions? In the United States, employees making under $100,000 do not put away enough money in order to provide for their twenty-plus years of retirement. Imagine trying to survive on some amount between $100,000 and $300,000 for *twenty-five years*. Yet this is the average projected retirement account for about a third of boomers once they stop making their contributions. It will not be enough – and people who rely on this money will soon find that they have to augment their incomes.

Second, in defined contribution plans the employer has turned the responsibility of managing retirement over to the employee. I think I am being fair when I say that most of us boomers simply do not have the planning capability or savvy to know how to manage our retirement portfolio. We tend to depend on "recommended" programs from employers or the hasty counsel of an "adviser." While sound and good investment programs exist, so does a plethora of bad ones. Retirement investments should yield about 7 percent annually, but most often we find programs that yield only minimal benefits. In order for these accounts to succeed, they have to be managed for maximum benefit for a number of years. Sadly, most of us are unaware of how our retirement programs are doing – and we're in for a big surprise when we are going to have to live on these accounts.

Finally, defined contribution plans have to provide a substantial return, so most of these plans are tied to the stock market. While over the long haul people usually gain money in the market, in the short term there can be profound volatility. Most stock portfolios lost at least one-third of their value after the 9/11 attacks. If you had reached retirement age right at that time, you would have found your resources substantially compromised. It is always important to remember that *defined contribution plans usually have no guaranteed benefit.*

"But wait!" you say. "Maybe there is one last hope out there for us and our retirement funds, courtesy of our government. After all, isn't that what Social Security and Medicare were created for — to provide a safety net for the aged workers of the United States?"

Let me say that I believe Social Security and Medicare will most likely survive to provide some benefits for boomers. My only uncertainty — and it's a big one — is that I don't know *how much* benefit will be available.

These programs face several challenges. When Social Security was created some seventy years ago, it was a "pay as you go" system. In other words, the current generation's workers would pay for the benefits given to the previous generation. This wasn't a problem when we had thirty-two workers for every person on Social Security; but since the program's inception, we have seen a dramatic drop in the ratio of workers to retirees. By the time the last of the boomers reach age sixty-five, the number of individuals in the aging population will move from 13 percent to almost 20 percent. During that same period, the number of workers will slightly decline. So instead of having almost five people working for every person of retirement age, we will have only three for every person over age sixty-five. The stark truth is that there will not be enough contribution from that working generation to supply all the needs of the retirement population. Because of these funding problems, Medicare is projected to be bankrupt by the year 2018, while Social Security is projected to be funded by only two-thirds the necessary levels by 2040.

In order for these programs to survive, benefits will likely be substantially cut. Most boomers will not receive full retirement benefits until a few years after age sixty-five. This trend is likely to expand in the future, when government benefits will likely kick in only after age seventy. In addition, the benefit amounts will likely be lower. If Medicare continues to exist, it will likely pay less, and boomers will be forced either to pay for supplemental health insurance or be directly responsible for more medical costs. In addition, Social Security will increasingly provide only a "supplement" of income. Currently, a person living only on Social Security is likely to fall below the poverty level. So even though these programs are likely to continue, boomers can expect a longer delay in receiving benefits and will receive fewer benefits when they finally do kick in.

The economic reality is clear: retirement for the boomer generation will be *very* different from that of the previous generation. Perhaps as many as half of us will find that our financial prospects in retirement will not be enough to keep us going for the twenty or thirty years we will live. Combine this with the stress that comes with providing financial help to our aging parents and adult children, and you see that a "life of leisure" is probably not in the cards. We will retire from our jobs, but we will likely have to augment our benefits with extra income. It will be the only way to make ends meet financially. We will be the generation that retires en masse, only to go back to work.

What Is God Doing with the Boomers?

We are poised to become the first Caregiving Generation, and I believe we will embrace the job, as we have embraced other "jobs" such as promoting civil rights, adjusting to computerization, and living as dual-career families.

But why us? Why now? We are a generation of people who have traditionally looked at life in terms of what makes us feel good. The hedonistic mantra of "if it feels good, do it!" originated out of our mouths.

Scripture, on the other hand, teaches us that life is not about feeling good or being happy; rather, it is about growth: "Do not conform any longer to the pattern of this world, but be transformed by the renewing of your mind. Then you will be able to test and approve what God's will is — his good, pleasing and perfect will" (Romans 12:2). The tap on the shoulder, if you will, is God commissioning us boomers for a work to be performed in this part of the twenty-first century. It isn't, however, only about loving and caregiving for our aging parents, instructing and guiding our adult children, or even learning how to cope with resources stretched to the maximum. It is about our growing into the image of Christ and learning how to be his people, eager to do his will.

Teaching Us to Be Loving and Humble

Caregiving challenges us to be loving and nurturing in ways we never thought possible. In many respects we are a generation of problem solvers who look at an issue — such as taking care of our elderly parents — as a series of assessments, interventions, and evaluations. In other words, we look at things in terms of what needs to be done and how we are to execute what needs getting done.

In the process of caring for our aging parents, however, something else totally transcends the process of problem solving. Caregiving is not so much about giving care as it is about us learning how to be loving and humble.

By the time our parents have aged and are in acute need of our care, they cannot overtly give anything back to us. They are dependent and weak and involved in the process of dying. Learning how to give and to love when we receive no obvious payback or benefit is the process of learning what *agapē* love (the kind of unconditional love the Bible talks about in 1 Corinthians 13) is all about. It takes great humility to do the task without demanding recognition.

If that kind of love sounds familiar, then you are on the right track. It is the kind of love that Jesus shows us when we find ourselves in despair over our own sinful status, unable to help ourselves:

Your attitude should be the same as that of Christ Jesus:

> Who, being in very nature God,
>> did not consider equality with God something
>>> to be grasped,
> but made himself nothing,
>> taking the very nature of a servant,
>> being made in human likeness.
> And being found in appearance as a man,
>> he humbled himself
>> and became obedient to death—
>>> even death on a cross!

Philippians 2:5–8

God is using the process of caregiving for our aging parents—and to a lesser extent, caring for our adult children—to shape and perfect in us this attitude of self-sacrificing love and humility. Back in the '60s, the Beatles once sang, "All you need is love." We all sang the song and honestly believed that love could change the world. And it really can—but only the kind of love born out of the hard work of sacrifice and humility. This kind of love is not easy to learn, but it has the power to transform our families and nourish our inner selves.

Teaching Us to Be Tough and Set Boundaries

While our generation has been masterful at adapting to change, we also have too often chased fads and the latest crazes. I believe that life has taught us boomers the art of self-control and discipline, as the overwhelming majority of us have come to grips with the fact that we must settle in and follow the rules of life to become responsible citizens and children of God. And we *are* responsible — but we haven't necessarily given up on the idea of "having it all."

Too often I fear we've fallen victim to the temptation to transfer the idea of having it all for ourselves to believing that our children should have it all. For that reason, we are not very good at teaching our children that they must adapt to a changing world and become responsible for themselves. It's as though we have been so caring and so adaptable that we think we can do it for our children, relieving them of the responsibility to be resourceful and solve problems for themselves. So when they leave high school or college, they feel perplexed over what to do next, because the world is not an easy place in which to "make it." In our efforts to help, we've done the hard work for them and have accepted them back into our homes or protected them from a variety of unpleasant situations.

Each generation must learn how to deal with the hard realities of its own era, because these realities are some of the main instruments God uses to modify and change our character. Our adult children are in the midst of having to learn valuable lessons about God and life, but they will learn only if we are willing to let them grow up and face their own issues. It's not that we do not love our children enough to give to them; we surely do. No, the crux of the matter is this: Can we learn to love our children enough to let them solve their own issues by letting them experience the natural consequences of their decisions? Can we be tough enough to set firm boundaries for our children and let them experience the pain and problems of natural consequences instead of stepping in and protecting them or bailing them out?

This attitude toward our children calls for a different kind of self-discipline that the boomer generation has yet to embrace. We haven't yet learned to set and keep a boundary strong enough to differentiate between issues that belong to our children and issues that belong to us. It will be a difficult proposition, as we have always wanted to protect them, but taking this approach is essential if our adult children are to grow into adulthood and become independent.

Sadly, most boomers have been wishy-washy at best on this issue of setting boundaries. It is not that we don't want our children to grow up; we just hate to experience the pain of watching them go through pain. We have to be tough enough with our pain to let our children experience their own.

The early church leader James wrote the following:

> If any of you lacks wisdom, he should ask God, who gives generously to all without finding fault, and it will be given to him. But when he asks, he must believe and not doubt, because he who doubts is like a wave of the sea, blown and tossed by the wind. That man should not think he will receive anything from the Lord; he is a double-minded man, unstable in all he does.
>
> James 1:5–8

We want the wisdom to know how to help our adult children through the difficult course ahead, learning how to be independent in a tough world. Surprise! To teach them this type of independence, we must be willing to *not* help them, or help them only in ways that will help them experience the consequences that teach them how to adapt, just as we once did. God is teaching not only them but also us to not be double-minded. We must learn to avoid running to the rescue or rushing to help whenever we feel the pain of our children's pain.

Teaching Us to Survive and Flourish

The people of Israel and Judah had a world of trouble inherited from their rebellious forefathers. They loved the land in which they lived and wished to stay there all their lives, but hostile nations surrounded them, especially the Assyrians and the Babylonians.

The Assyrians struck first, carting away the whole northern kingdom of Israel. More than a century later, the Babylonians invaded Judah, conquered it, and shipped a large number of its inhabitants off to Babylon. There they languished, and the report from the prophet Jeremiah was not good. They were going to be stuck there for generations.

All of them felt hungry for some morsel of good news. It finally came, but by means of some false prophets, who declared the exile would last only a few months. Soon, they said, the displaced people of Judah would be allowed to return to their homeland.

Who among us doesn't long for such a pleasant message? We boomers hear all the bad news about our crumbling Social Security, Medicare, and pension benefits, and it's enough to make us wish we could just skip over the next couple of decades and die in peace. But the hard times *are* coming and *will not* go away. We cannot avoid the issues of the coming financial storms, at least not in the near future. Increasing numbers of us will see our planned lifestyles curtailed, and about one-third of us will lack the necessary resources to survive on what we have saved. We will have to go back to work, and many of us will struggle to work in our very old age. It does not sound fun, and it certainly does not sound like anything we would willingly go through.

Yet listen to Jeremiah: "This is what the LORD says: Do not listen to the prophets who say, 'Very soon now the articles from the LORD's house will be brought back from Babylon.' They are prophesying lies to you. Do not listen to them. Serve the king of Babylon, and you will live" (Jeremiah 27:16–17). The old prophet was essentially telling his people that the bad times would continue, so they should set their minds on working, serving, and living. It might not be fun or satisfying work, and it certainly wasn't in a place where they wished to be. But God intended to keep them in Babylon for a long time, and if they wanted to survive, they had to live and work on the banks of the hated Kebar.

Likewise, we boomers may long to escape the hassles ahead of us, but I believe God is saying, "This is your hard time to go through." To focus on escaping the hard time means that we descend into a foolish waiting game, longing for the happiness that we hope different circumstances will bring. This kind of waiting produces not wisdom, but whining. God does not want us merely to live through the next few decades of scarce resources and hard work; he wants us to live and to learn about him and about how to flourish even under difficult circumstances. Not everything that lies ahead of us is good, but all things can work for our wisdom and learning:

> We know that in all things God works for the good of those who love him, who have been called according to his purpose. For those God foreknew he also predestined to be conformed to the likeness of his Son that he might be the firstborn among many brothers.
>
> Romans 8:28–29

I do not know all that we will learn from the difficulties of our coming retirement, but perhaps over everything else we will grasp the value of relationships. Perhaps we will learn that loyalty, faithfulness, and courage are much more reliable and valuable than our bank accounts or retirement portfolios. Perhaps we will learn that the new insights we gain and the joy we experience as we love our families on the edge of existence are far better than the pain of losing each other in the pursuit of the comforts of our own indulgences and selfish desires. God is going to be working through the hard times in our retirement and our years of aging. We can complain about how difficult it is, or we can cooperate with how it is going to change us for the better.

What is God doing in bringing these three issues together for us? Frankly, I'm not sure. But I am convinced of two things: God is at work, and God wants the boomer generation to change to become more like his Son, Jesus.

God always has used people and events to do the really big things that have altered the course of a generation and the course of human history. Will the boomers on the edge of these epic changes produce something that big? I do not know how big it will be, but I know this present time has all the hallmarks of a radical opportunity to change the way people think and do things—which means a radical opportunity to help both ourselves and others more clearly recognize that the kingdom of God is at hand.

We are the Caregiving Generation. Let us embrace the future and everything there is to learn about ourselves, as well as how we can better navigate our way through these three onrushing realities.

PART 1

THE
CHALLENGE
OF

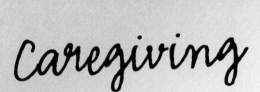

Caregiving

DID YOU SAY "CAREGIVING"?

Let me be clear: aging is not optional. Most of us think, "Yeah, I know I'm getting older, and I'm beginning to feel all the creaks and aches that signal the reality that my body is changing and falling apart, a little at a time." While true, this isn't exactly what I mean.

When I say the word *aging*, I mean the time of life when disease or wear takes a toll on the body big enough to significantly diminish or remove entirely a person's ability to function independently. Certainly, all of us are getting older, but not all of us are counted among the aging population.

Our chronological age is no longer a predictable marker of when we will hit this aging category. It certainly is not when we receive our AARP cards. It is doubtful it will be when we reach the traditional retirement age of sixty-five. And most likely it will not even be once we reach our seventies, when most of us will still be performing activities that look very much like middle age.

You see, when I say *aging*, I really mean the group that some may call the "old, old." This group of people can no longer hold on to their lives without some significant help from outsiders. Aging means giving up on the pretense that life will go on forever and accepting that death may be right around the corner. Aging means that health, wealth, and even relationships start to slip from one's grasp, like a ship sailing away that grows smaller and dimmer and eventually disappears over the horizon.

This is the group that is revolutionizing aging as we know it. All of us boomers will eventually reach this "aging" category, but for the time being, we are simply getting older in our "middle age." It is our parents who are now slipping into this "aging" group, and many are no longer able to manage everyday activities by themselves.

If you are not currently caring for an aging parent or in-law, chances are that you have started seeing some telltale signs that the decline of aging is at hand. As we have seen, medical science can keep people alive for many years, even when they have severe chronic health problems such as heart disease and emphysema. So with the advancement of medical science, not only do people live longer and healthier than at any other time in history; they also live longer and *un*healthier than at any time in history.

For most, aging will mean a slow decline to eventual death. More and more help will be required with financial, emotional, and physical issues. I do not mean to refer to aging as some sort of macabre "death march," because this process can bring some of the sweetest and most meaningful connections one can experience, where wisdom, courage, and strength become most evident. But aging is a time of decline, a long pathway to an eventual passing out of this life into the next. And with that decline comes the inevitable need for assistance and caregiving.

And who will do this caregiving? Those of us who are in the boomer age group, of course. More than 90 percent of the care given to elders is provided by their families. Some elders need twenty-four-hour care and have medical problems that demand a nursing or care facility, but only about 5 to 8 percent of the aging population occupies one of these institutional facilities at any one time. And even if the elder is at a care facility, the caregiving responsibility remains, with families providing financial support and management, regular emotional connection, and, most of the time, augmenting the physical care provided by the institution.

The whole process of dealing with the decline of our elders—modifying their home environment, getting them to the proper medical treatment, managing and anticipating their care needs, and negotiating the switch of power and control of finances and decision making—is all part of the caregiving process, which, as mentioned earlier, can last a decade or more. Again, who will do this caregiving? It has been and will continue to be the boomer generation—and it is the first reality that will change the lives of boomers forever.

The Worthy Woman Named Genevieve

Several years ago, my wife and I began the process of caring for my mother-in-law, Genevieve. Genevieve was remarkable in so many ways. She had married an advertising executive from southern California when she was twenty-one, and she gave birth to four children in the next ten years. Her husband, Bill, was a "bigger than life" character with boundless energy and creativity. They ran with a beautiful crowd in Hollywood and had what many would consider "the good life."

But Bill suffered from bipolar disorder and struggled mightily with severe bouts of depression throughout his life. During one such depressive episode, he made the tragic decision to take his own life.

With four children, Genevieve made the courageous decision to move her family to Texas, where one of her brothers lived. Somehow she managed to pull her life back together. She galvanized herself against her own pain and set about getting her children in school and making a new life.

But a year later, tragedy struck once again when her oldest son, Bruce, became ill and suddenly died from acute leukemia. Surely she felt stunned beyond measure to lose both a husband and son within such a short period, but she kept moving and faithfully poured herself into her two remaining sons and her only daughter.

What seems most remarkable to me is that my wife remembers her growing-up years as characterized by happiness and filled with laughter. She recalls two tennis-playing big brothers and a loving mother who worked to create a healthy and nurturing household. Somehow, this worthy woman named Genevieve was able to overcome her personal pain to shore up the lives of her children and give them a happy home.

But her tragic story was not over. When her oldest remaining son was a senior in college, he and his date did not return from an evening out one Saturday night. A search the next day revealed that they had fallen victim to a brutal murderer who had locked their bodies in the trunk of her son's car.

Many people lose half of their family members to tragedy, but very few lose them at different times in such painful ways. When Genevieve found her family of six reduced to three, how did she survive? She focused on what was ahead and not on what was behind. She raised her two remaining children to adulthood; saw both of them graduate from college and earn advanced degrees; rejoiced as they found love and married; beamed as they fathered and mothered her grandchildren. Together, the family of three grew into close relationships with one another, deep and resourceful relationships with God, and generative relationships with spouses and offspring. In many ways, it wasn't just a matter of surviving the tragedy; hurts were actually healed.

But everything wasn't perfect. Genevieve always had a secret coping mechanism that, while understandable, peppered the decades with some unhappy and unfortunate times. When she was in pain or experiencing terrible loneliness, she would drink. Occasionally at first, but as her isolation and loneliness grew with age, she began to drink more and more.

Then came one final blow. Twenty years after the murder of her son, a suspect was brought to trial. Although no new evidence had been uncovered, and old evidence had been destroyed, an overzealous district attorney and a police department desiring to clear its name brought the case to trial. It was as if the family had been thrown back into an ancient foxhole in a battle that it had thought was long over. But once again, the family had to face all the gruesome details, painful reminders, and harsh realities of how some deranged killer had cut short the life of a vivacious and loving son. After months of revisiting awful details and experiencing a useless trial that ended in a "not guilty" verdict, Genevieve and her family had been victimized by the tragedy all over again. This time, however, it seemed too much for this remarkable woman, and she began to slip into the oblivion of her alcoholism and isolation.

At the time, I had a great job as an assistant professor at a university where I loved to teach. But my wife and I saw firsthand how the emotional pain of the trial, followed by the uncontrolled alcoholism, was making Genevieve's life disappear. We made the decision to move back to Texas to look after Genevieve. I took a job at a fine community college, but I never found the job as fulfilling as my former teaching responsibilities or my research projects. Still, I reasoned that we were going to help Genevieve over the rough spots in this time of trouble, and then God would send us on our way to another university.

But we soon discovered the breadth of Genevieve's isolation that fed her anxiety, which led her to drink more—finally triggering the big "A": Alzheimer's disease. In her illness, Genevieve resisted our efforts to help her and slid more and more toward the icy place of frozen thoughts, disappearing memory, and the despair of dementia. This prompted desperation of our own as we tried to care for a woman who would not accept care and as I dealt with a position where I felt increasingly unfulfilled and unhappy.

I had been willing to accept my new job when I believed that Genevieve would respond gratefully to our care and I would soon move on with my promising career. But when it became clear that Genevieve was not going to get stable, let alone better, and that moving to a community college had essentially cut off my university-level career, I really began questioning what God was doing. I began to resent God for sticking me in a place where I saw no way of escape and little challenge or good that I was accomplishing. Genevieve slid into the long and slow dying process of Alzheimer's, while I remained stuck in a job I disliked in a place I hated. Certainly, many things in my life were good. My wife and I related well, and my children prospered. But the constant drain of feeling stuck was enough to push me over into the abyss of depression.

Maybe not all boomer caregivers land in depression while marching through the course of caregiving, but many of us land where I did, when I wondered just what God was doing in my life. For the most part, we expect that our lives will move forward in productive ways, resulting in our happiness. But the job of caregiving challenges that notion to the very core.

As boomers, we have plans for our lives: seeing our kids grow up and have kids of their own, and seeing our lineage grow; achieving financial security and occupational stability; finally slowing down and reaping some of the harvest of the long years of work and raising our families. All of these things seem to be the "self-evident" plan of God.

But caregiving is like a wrench thrown into the mechanics of this perfect plan. We begin to see that the involvement and care we thought we would be giving to grandchildren is being spent instead in caregiving to Mom or Dad. We lurch into the reality that we may have to work for many more years in order to provide for the financial needs that Mom or Dad cannot cover. We may realize that the priority we once gave to our work is compromised as we have to spend more time caregiving – a reality that may result in less and less job security. And we get hit hard with the prognosis that a good part of the restful life we anticipated is going to become busier than ever before as we spend our lives in caregiving.

Most of us boomers are willing, at first, to take on the job. But as the reality soaks in that our lives will be changed for a long time – doing a task that may not be well received and that inevitably results in the continued decline of our loved one – we become less keen on our prospects. We know that our elders need care – but how are we as boomers to make sense of the task before us and actually make sure that it fulfills the purpose God intends?

Three Biblical Guidelines for Caregiving

As it is with anything that involves significant issues, we should first respond by going to Scripture for answers. Unfortunately, the concept of aging found in the Bible bears little resemblance to the process we face today.

In biblical days, people remained fairly active until they hit the wall of some ailment, illness, or injury that put their lives in danger. Once such problems occurred, given the limits of ancient medical care and knowledge, the elders usually died in short order. Loved ones surely gave them care in terms of basic nurture but had little to offer in the way of treatment.

Though there is a lack of clear and specific biblical instruction regarding the process of caregiving for an aging family member, I have found three general principles that provide both help and counsel.

PRINCIPLE 1: Responsibility

Exodus 20:12 presents the consummate idea of *responsibility* toward our parents: "Honor your father and your mother, so that you may live long in the land the LORD your God is giving you." Here we find what seems to be a straightforward command from God to honor our parents. How? By listening to what they say, respecting who they are, and caring for their needs. In turn, we are promised that our obedience will be rewarded with a long and fruitful life. While I believe this is the basic thrust of the verse, I also think there is a much deeper meaning to grasp.

When my mother-in-law was declining rapidly with dementia, it became clear to all of us that her nutrition was also deteriorating rapidly. She seldom ate anything that resembled a real meal and typically survived on snack crackers. My wife, Sharon, and I would fix meals for her and take them to her house, but she would become angry at what she saw as an unwelcome intrusion. Soon she began refusing any meals we brought. Nor would she accept any help from Meals on Wheels, believing that those types of services were meant for people who were "old" or "in need," but certainly not her. It became clear to us that she would have to move into an apartment complex that offered some type of meal service.

When we brought up the subject of a possible move, she either vehemently refused to discuss it or adopted a scowling stonewalling tactic. When we persisted, she insisted that we should leave her alone and let her live however she wanted to live.

Many caregivers who deal with similar conversations know the rough terrain of trying to reason with an elder who wants to hold on to houses, apartments, cars, independence, and familiar ways. We want to honor our fathers and mothers in keeping with the biblical command—but how can we do what they want (or order us to do) when we know it will harm them? Is that what "honoring" is about?

I don't think so. The fact is, there comes a time in many elders' lives where the caregiving adult children know what is best—much more than the deteriorating elders do. Despite the claim that "I know how to take care of myself," or "I know what's best for me," it is undeniable that the caregiver can see much more clearly what is in the best physical and emotional interest of the elder. It is also true that the caregiver can often see what is in the best interest of the entire family, as the group struggles to keep up with the various demands of life even while integrating the care of an older member.

We will certainly butt heads with our aging parents over care issues. Many times! Sometimes it will be over simple issues such as bathing, going to the doctor, or brushing teeth. Sometimes it will be over complex and heavy issues such as moving, driving, or managing finances. We need to honor and respect them in the way we listen to their concerns, but in the end, the caregiver usually does know what is best. If we move forward in a respectful and informed way, then I believe we are still fulfilling the biblical command to honor our parents.

Remember, the elder also has a responsibility in the family. The care receiver must be willing to receive the needed care in order to make the caregiving job both effective and efficient.

There is a rhythm to the cycle of family life. There is a time when we stand front and center on life's stage, with all the lights shining on us. Typically, this takes place when we marry and start to have children. But as these children grow and begin to take their own places at center stage, we find that we get forced off to the side to serve in supporting roles. As our children raise their children and these newest members of the clan claim center stage, we find our role even further diminished as the cycle of family life moves forward to other generations. If we make the transition well, however, we support the entire process and strengthen the legacy of the family. When death finally overtakes us and we make our final exit from the stage, our families will applaud and remember us as giving, supportive, and much beloved players.

How sad, then, to see a family where the rhythm gets very much thrown off. Instead of raising their children to take center stage, a parent may muscle the children aside, demanding that his or her needs take precedence. Instead of supporting the needs of future generations, the person continues to demand center stage and insist that the younger generations serve him or her and make him or her happy. We've all seen this type of person—and we've witnessed the enormous problems it causes families. The fact is, however, that this person will also die and make a final exit from the stage of life. But when such a person dies, the family does not applaud; rather, one can hear a collective sigh of relief, exposing a barely concealed delight that the nightmare has finally ended.

A care receiver who does not join with the caregiver in this braided cord of caregiving by being willing to accept and receive care runs the risk of becoming one of these "center stage" actors who throws off the family cycle. The elder in need of care has to realize that his or her needs comprise only part of the story of "living long in the land." In order for the generational lineage of the family to be strengthened and made healthy, the elder must be connected, malleable, and respectful of how caregiving fits the entire extended family. This idea of connection is the heart of the biblical command to honor one's father and mother. It is *not* simply about doing what a parent says but rather about how to be connected, realizing that the generational process is about strengthening families.

As caregivers, we honor and work to stay connected to our older parents because in this way we demonstrate to our children that love and value ultimately reside in relationship rather than in work or money. We learn this drill best in a sound family where relationships get built over a span of time. However frail and needy our family members may be, we stay connected to them and honor them because of the wisdom and emotional strength they offer. We do not learn this perseverance and commitment through shallow relationships. In shallow relationships, when times are hard or demands are too much, we simply move on. God wants us to stay connected in our family relationships over the long haul, no matter what the cost.

But again, "honoring" cannot be accomplished by the caregiver alone. The elder must be willing to stay connected, which doesn't require the elder to just shut up and take whatever the caregiver suggests or demands. But caregiver and care receiver must work together to listen and formulate plans that effectively provide the care needed while ultimately making connection more possible and meaningful.

We have the responsibility to honor and care for parents as they grow old, but we need to be clear on what that responsibility entails. It does not entail the elder's right to demand anything he or she wishes, to manipulate promises or agreements on future care, or to treat offspring in insensitive or disrespectful ways. Honoring does not mean that the caregiver does exactly what the aging parent says, but neither does it mean that caregivers always have the "trump card" to make the aging parent do whatever they demand. This responsibility is best carried out when both are intertwined in a mutual band of honor and respect and committed to do what is best for the long-term interests of the whole family. This is how families are made stronger by caregiving and how they learn eventually to "live long in the land."

PRINCIPLE 2: Openhandedness

Many Bible passages speak about the obligation to care for the poor or someone in need, but I like these Deuteronomy verses the best: "If there is a poor man among your brothers in any of the towns of the land that the LORD your God is giving you, do not be hardhearted or tightfisted toward your poor brother. Rather be openhanded and freely lend him whatever he needs" (Deuteronomy 15:7–8). I love these verses because the concept of "tightfisted" seems to fit the stress, anxiety, and anger that seem so pervasive in our society.

Tightfisted Due to Stress

Although the fall made us both sinful and selfish, most people are natural givers to their families. Something bad usually has to happen in order for us to disengage from giving to a family member.

One big reason we stop giving and become "tightfisted" is simply the feeling we have of being overwhelmed by the press of so many things in our lives. Work, home, children, grandchildren, church, and community obligations pile up on us to the point where most of us feel we work as hard as possible and we're still unable to complete all the tasks before us. We get used to the idea that certain activities have to be squeezed out now and then, such as not participating in church during certain seasons or letting home projects slip behind. Most of us, however, will keep up the juggling act and eventually will get to most of the things that need to be done.

But when a job like caregiving for an aging parent comes along, it is difficult indeed to see how everything can continue to get done. We quickly see that caregiving can consume significant portions of our lives, perhaps even taking 50 percent or more of our time—and usually it's time we don't think we can spare. As a result, we tend to protect ourselves from the caregiving task by putting ourselves into a state of denial ("Mom or Dad really can manage OK," or "I know God will take care of them") or "punting" the caregiving ball to someone else in the family.

Without question, we are a stressed-out society. There is no good time to take on the financial burden of caregiving, miss the ballgames or special events of children or grandchildren, pass over important relationships, or put pressing matters on hold. But all of these things and more will happen when we take on the job of being openhanded in caregiving.

Remember, we will always be under stress. Think of these words from the apostle Paul: "We have this treasure in jars of clay to show that this all-surpassing power is from God and not from us. We are hard pressed on every side, but not crushed; perplexed, but not in despair; persecuted, but not abandoned; struck down, but not destroyed" (2 Corinthians 4:7–9). The power of God by which we live does not guarantee us a life free from stress, but rather that we will be able to maintain and persist in the midst of stress. When just thinking about the big job of caregiving overwhelms us, we need to remember that we do not have to face the job a decade at a time, a year at a time, or even a day at a time. We face it one moment at a time.

In the midst of a particularly hard stretch of life, where Sharon and I were facing the press of seeing too many clients in our practices, going to too many activities with our children, and meeting the obligations of writing, teaching, speaking, and living life, Genevieve fell and broke her wrist. We certainly did not have time to get her to the emergency room for X-rays, meet with the orthopedic surgeon, schedule and go through surgery, and work through several follow-up appointments and rehabilitation sessions. But somehow, in the crush of everything we had to do, we accomplished all of those things – and Genevieve's wrist was repaired. How did we do it? I don't mean to oversimplify, but we did it by continuing to move ahead and do the next thing. Did things suffer? I'm sure that they did. But in the long run, we moved through a difficult caregiving stretch, loaded with stress from various directions, and came out the other side. We simply received the grace to do the next thing in front of us.

Even in the midst of stress, we focus *on the need at hand*, and, with an open hand, take care of the next obligation.

Tightfisted Due to Anxiety

Sometimes we become tightfisted because we do not believe we have what it takes to do the job of caregiving. We grow anxious that somehow we will either mess up the job or be incompetent at doing what needs to be done. Few caregivers are unfamiliar with this type of anxiety.

There is so much we have to know in terms of medical conditions, legal mechanics, communication and service organizations, as well as being able to competently negotiate with our elder. And let's be honest, investing a good portion of our time doesn't guarantee success in getting problems solved. And in the end, nothing we do can prevent the death of our aging parent. Many times, it can feel as though we are simply caregiving failures – and all of this failure to "make it all better" can add up and make us feel inadequate, incapable, and incompetent. Thus, we can quickly come to the conclusion that we do not measure up as human beings. And that makes us feel anxious.

Make no mistake, you will respond with anxiety and fear. You may spin into deep bouts of depression, have fits of rage, be hypervigilant in trying to control every detail around you, or descend into the chaotic hopelessness of running from every obligation. In short, you will occasionally depart from the peaceful and consistent giving that caregiving demands.

How do we remain openhanded in the midst of the anxiety of caregiving? It is essential to remember that our worth as caregivers is not tied to "success" but to *who we are in Christ*. When people in Jesus' day looked at his ministry, many must have judged it to be an utter failure. He held unorganized meetings, and his overall strategy seemed unplanned and at times ineffective. But Jesus wasn't about a plan of ministry or strategies for success; he was about the business of connecting through relationships. More than anything else, he judged as most important his power to connect and to bring individuals to a saving knowledge of himself.

Following the lead of Jesus means we do not judge ourselves by whether we make all the right caregiving decisions or whether our aging parent likes us or treats us well or whether we make progress in addressing the various ailments that befall our elder. Rather, our success is tied to how much we seek to give ourselves in loving service. More often than not, this condition of giving our heart with the intention of doing good will result in sound and trustworthy connection with our aging parent. And Paul's testimony will be ours: "In all these things we are more than conquerors through [Christ] who loved us" (Romans 8:37).

Tightfisted Due to Anger

Many of us have difficulty with being openhanded in the process of caregiving for an aging parent because of our struggles with anger. Sometimes we are angry because we think it is unfair that our siblings fail to do their fair share in shouldering the caregiving load. This is a difficult subject, because such a failure really *isn't* fair — and anger is the natural response.

Most of us did not volunteer for the job of caregiving; we received the job either because we were the closest in geographical proximity, the closest to our parents emotionally, or the weakest in being able to refuse the job. While we are left to hold the caregiving bag, our siblings are off living their lives, with what looks to be just the "normal" cares of the world.

I believe it is important to face this issue head-on, and there are three factors that enter into the discussion. First, our society is very mobile; that fact alone makes it very unlikely that more than one sibling will reside close enough to aging parents to provide the necessary caregiving. It is not unusual for siblings to live hundreds, if not thousands, of miles from aging parents. Second, aging parents often *prefer* or *trust* one sibling above another, which doesn't necessarily mean they have a favorite or are emotionally partial to a particular child. Most often, aging parents just know who is best equipped to provide the caregiving. Finally, siblings aren't likely to reach total agreement on the variety of issues that surround caregiving, yet those decisions must be made and implemented in a timely fashion.

These three facts have led me to see that caregiving "by committee" — trying to share the caregiving load among several siblings — usually does not work. If it works in your family, then by all means continue to use this approach. But for most families, *one primary caregiver* should be the preferred mode of operation.

I make this suggestion for two reasons. First, it is important to have decision making, financial control, and caregiving vested in the same person. Far too often, I've seen a well-meaning caregiver try to authorize a medical procedure or facilitate a move to a care facility for an aging parent, only to have the sibling who manages the finances refuse to pay for what the caregiver believes to be in the best interest of the parent. Even though the job is big, dividing it up often results in separating *power* from *responsibility*. I believe that the individual who has the responsibility to care for the parent also needs the financial control and decision-making power necessary to get the job done. To do anything else makes for ineffective caregiving and thrusts additional unfairness on the caregiver.

Second, I recommend this "one primary caregiver" model because it frees siblings and other family members to fulfill a necessary and important role in the caregiving process. You see, caregivers are significantly taxed by the job responsibilities. Research tells us that caregivers have a higher rate of depression, poorer health, and more relational difficulties in their families. It is a *very* stressful job, and caregivers traditionally don't take good care of themselves. Siblings and other family members who cannot serve as the primary caregiver can still be a part of the primary caregiver's *support group*.

Very simply, this support group gives care to the caregiver. Its main function is to make sure that the caregiver gets the support, respite, and care needed to bear the heavy load. For instance, instead of a sibling trying to "share" the caregiving, he or she could perhaps come twice a year to give the primary caregiver respite away from the job or time to travel. Those who live near the caregiver could provide daily opportunities for the caregiver to attend an exercise or yoga class. While such assistance may also allow for direct caregiving for an elder, the focus is not on providing eldercare as much as it is on providing the caregiver with much needed care. Other examples include providing money so that the caregiver's house can be cleaned or maintained, making supportive calls to connect with and enjoy the caregiver, or planning vacations or time off to be available to support the caregiver.

But even with this model, the reality remains: much of the responsibilities and stress of caregiving rest with one person. We can make excuses and wish that things were different, but the reality is that the elderly will live longer in sickness than ever before. The government does not and will not have the resources to provide long-term care for our aging population. Social services are stretched to the maximum in most communities, not even coming close to meeting the current needs. So the care of an aging parent *will* fall to an adult child. If that adult child is you – whether your siblings or your parent wanted you to have the job – the job is yours. It may be unfair, but you will do much better if you embrace the responsibility of caregiving, secure the power necessary to execute the job, and get the support you need to take care of yourself.

"But I'm not angry with my siblings," someone protests. That's wonderful. But are you angry with your parents? Many caregivers are.

Perhaps you were treated badly or not nurtured by your parents, or maybe you were neglected or abused emotionally, verbally, or sexually. Whatever the reason for your anger, you tried to put distance between you and the past – and now you find that your aging parent needs you to provide care. Here you are, forced to provide care to a parent who did not provide care for you as a child or, worse yet, damaged or took advantage of you when you could not protect yourself. Your heart cries out, "How *dare* you ask me for care now! You didn't care for me when *I* needed it!"

Although in such a reality it is difficult to be openhanded with caregiving, it is not impossible. First, give yourself permission to stay angry. Many will lob Bible verses at you, urging you to deny your anger, referring you to Jesus' command to turn the other cheek (see Matthew 5:39) or to forgive if you want to be forgiven (see Matthew 6:14; 18:35). You will ultimately give better care and open the door for improved relationships if you first allow yourself the grace to stay where you are emotionally instead of trying to manipulate yourself into happy or joyful giving. You cannot obligate your heart into forgetting the injustices done to you by a destructive or irresponsible parent. Your heart wants justice, and justice isn't a bad thing. But somewhere in your heart, too, you know this parent possesses the very thing that can heal your heart — whether it is showing love, admitting wrong, apologizing, or asking for forgiveness.

Second, make sure you set up secure and substantial boundaries with that elder. Many times, aging parents in need of care use the same relationship tricks they've used all their lives, such as yelling, growing angry, manipulating, or getting physical. Setting boundaries sometimes means not responding to a request stated in anger; sometimes it means ignoring manipulative statements and withdrawing; sometimes it means confronting the behavior. Setting boundaries with a damaging or irresponsible aging parent means that you control your own emotions and do not allow yourself to get trapped into a hurtful web of behavior. Illegitimate approval seeking can end up facilitating the elder's dysfunctional actions.

Third, seek out the aging parent's story. Many times, the elder was also a victim of neglect or abuse. While this past reality doesn't excuse the hurtful behavior or irresponsibility done to you, the understanding that an aging parent was damaged and has many of the same feelings you have can often facilitate a human connection. Once we hear the story of the elder, we often recognize that if we had been in his or her situation, saddled with his or her limitations, we probably wouldn't have done much better. This in turn makes us realize that the irresponsible or unloving acts did not come from an unfeeling "monster" who hated us for some unknown reason, but from a damaged human being who made unfortunate and damaging choices to cope with a hurtful past—choices we might have made had we been in the same situation. Again, this doesn't excuse the elder from responsibility, but it does tend to help us reduce the anger that makes us tightfisted in our giving.

I like to remind people there is always a chance that God will choose to work a miracle in hearts and so bring about reconciliation and healing. Hurts and wrongs that have festered for decades very often revert to open wounds when the call comes to care for an aging parent. But with the reopening of that wound also comes new opportunities to do something different.

Josey was forced to care for her elderly father, a man who had been physically abusive and alcoholic during her childhood. In those frequent times when he came home drunk and in a rage, he would beat up his wife. By the time Josey had become a teenager, he had abandoned the home, even though he would sometimes show up at important events, such as birthdays and graduations—more often than not, embarrassing her by coming drunk. She swore she was through with him and had seen him less than a half a dozen times after she had left home, married, and raised her daughter and son. But when the call came that he was dying of lung cancer, she agreed to take him to appointments and help him get his affairs in order.

For a good part of the seven months she gave her dying father care, nothing differed in their relationship. She would silently come in and do what needed to be done. They would talk a bit about his illness and care, but they never touched on the past or on any intimate issues.

"I was just too angry about all that had gone on," Josey explained. "I looked at the process as something I had to go through as a responsibility, but I resented every moment of having to care for him, because he had never cared for me."

But about a month before her father died, he surprised her by saying something totally unexpected—and completely different.

"You've had no reason to take care of me like you have these past several months, and I want you to know I appreciate it," he blurted out one day. Josey felt stunned and simply looked at him for several minutes.

"The anger that had built up inside of me over all those years was just ready to explode," she admitted. She shared with me her response: "I said to him, 'Thank you for that, but it isn't enough to make everything right between us. If you want to talk about the issues between us, then we will talk. If you don't, then don't bring it up again.'"

To her surprise, her father *did* want to talk. "He talked for nearly two days straight. It was more like a confession," Josey said. After so much confession, Josey finally asked her father, "What do you want from me?"

"I don't really want anything from you," he replied. "I just wanted you to know that I recognize now what I didn't give you. I'm sorry for that."

And with those words, Josey said, "somehow almost all my anger just sloughed off. I stared into his eyes and I knew that he meant what he said. I took his hand, kissed him on the cheek, and said, 'That feels much better to me.' Then he took my hand and said that he loved me. I was a bit stunned to hear what fell out of my mouth. I said, 'I love you too, Daddy.' I don't know that I had ever called him Daddy in my whole life. But here we were, at the end of his life, after so much anger and hate, saying that we loved each other. My heart that had been sealed off from him was healed by that one experience."

Certainly not all experiences are like Josey's. Sometimes caregivers watch their aging parents take to their graves many of the hurtful issues they lived with for years. But working through anger to be even a *little* openhanded with your caregiving can open new relationship possibilities. Many times, those new possibilities result in reconnection, reconciliation, and healing.

PRINCIPLE 3: Evenness

Sometimes the first two principles of *responsibility* and *openhanded-ness* can seem overwhelming, because they lean so much toward giving. The third principle, *evenness*, reminds us that balance is necessary.

I see this principle described in two passages of Scripture. The first is found in the gospel of Luke: "Yet the news about [Jesus] spread all the more, so that crowds of people came to hear him and to be healed of their sicknesses. But Jesus often withdrew to lonely places and prayed" (5:15–16). As the word spread about Jesus and his miraculous healing powers, crowds pressed in on him. Someone in great need always stood before him. Yet, even in such an environment of overwhelming needs, he took the time to nurture his own individuality and spiritual connection with his Father.

The second passage describes how a "disciple-wannabe" asked to be temporarily excused from following Jesus so that he could go and bury his father. "Let the dead bury their own dead, but you go and proclaim the kingdom of God," Jesus said (Luke 9:60). At first glance, Jesus' words appear harsh and unfeeling. But Jesus was simply stating that some work in the kingdom of God differs from the work of caring for family.

Caregiving is a consuming job. The physical deterioration of our elder means there is always something to do—a bill to pay, an appointment to make, a shopping list to complete, a bath to give. The list can go on and on, with new issues continually on the horizon. If we are not careful, we can begin to focus exclusively on being a problem solver for our aging parent. As additional problems appear, more and more of our lives become consumed by the problems.

Let me be clear: God does want us to take responsibility for the caregiving of our aging parents, and he does want us to remain openhanded in the way we go about meeting their needs. But we must never forget that God also expects us to take care of our other roles and responsibilities. Only then can we be healthy caregivers.

While evenness and balance in caregiving have many facets, I'll focus here on two issues in particular. The first issue concerns your own spiritual life and physical life.

When you become responsible for another human being, it's easy to see yourself as a person who must have all the answers and meet all the needs. Since an aging parent often expects his or her caregiver to meet all needs, the caregiver often adopts exactly that role. With so much control and responsibility, we begin to see ourselves as some kind of "support reservoir," as though all things needed for life will flow from us. But in order to be a reservoir, we must be in contact with a supply for our own replenishment—and that truth is easy to forget.

If you're going to take on the job of caregiving, you must first be committed to taking care of yourself. You should have two to three good relationships that nurture and revitalize you. You must have a weekly plan for physically caring for yourself. You need to take regular time away from caregiving to rest and relax. And most important, you must have a daily and weekly plan to get spiritual nurture into your life. For many, to do so will involve daily quiet times, weekly Bible studies, fellowship with other believers, and regular worship. This is not being selfish! Jesus knew that if he did not care for himself, he would have nothing to give to the masses. In the same way, if you don't take care of yourself, you'll have nothing to give as a caregiver.

Many caregivers give of themselves completely, paying no attention to their own physical and spiritual needs. They wear themselves down to the physical and emotional nub—and then find they can no longer bear the responsibility of caregiving. If this happens to you, you will not only ruin your own health and spiritual well-being; you'll also place your elder at risk. It is not a selfish thing to take care of yourself! It is utterly necessary. Remember this: if you go down, your aging parent will go down with you.

The second crucial issue regarding evenness concerns your other roles in life. Caregiving often presses on you from every side. So many issues need to be taken care of—from ordering and dispensing medications to paying bills. The press of all these issues can lead to a kind of tyranny that will never let you rest. The truth is that there is *always* something more that needs to be done, and this press will tend to squeeze out some very important things.

I am always amazed at how much time we caregivers spend doing "things" and how little time we spend connecting with people. This is true even with connecting with our elder. We get so busy taking care of bathing, medications, cleaning, and dressing that we spend no time laughing, holding, and having intimate conversations. And if we have this tendency with the elder (for whom we are giving so much care), just imagine how often we do this with our spouses, our children, and our grandchildren!

I believe God has commissioned the boomer generation to be caregivers in this epoch of history. I believe we will become a caregiving generation that is both unselfish and generous. I believe it is for our good that we have this responsibility and that we will set the standard and example for generations to follow.

But I also believe we have other jobs and responsibilities. We are to be good spouses and have long walks and loving times with the loves of our lives. We are to be good parents as we watch our children grow into adulthood and as we take time to pass along our wisdom to them. And we are to be good grandparents as we bequeath God's precious gifts of identity and love. In order to do these things, however, we're going to end up letting some problems go unsolved. Maybe it will mean paying a bill late or skipping a bath, missing an appointment or delaying a medication time. You must give yourself the grace to let some of these problems slip through the cracks. If you don't, the tyranny of caregiving will wipe out your ability to make meaningful connections and to fulfill all the other roles God has given you.

These are the three great principles of caregiving: responsibility, openhandedness, and evenness. There is no list of rules to follow, and an effective application of these principles demands balance and a learning heart. Without a doubt, caregiving changed *my* heart.

God Changes Us
into the Caregiving Generation

I used to think I was some kind of hero for deciding to come back to Texas to take care of my mother-in-law. I thought I would give her the care she needed, she would express her appreciation, I would get a pat on the back and soon be on my way again, secure in the knowledge that I had sacrificed and given when God told me to do so. But Genevieve was very difficult to care for. She didn't appreciate my sacrifices. And I got stuck for a long time in a place I had no desire to be in.

But I was also stuck emotionally. I was mad at Genevieve, mad at God, and depressed about my circumstances. When I didn't see how anything in my life was going to change appreciably, I settled in to ride out the unhappy time as best I could.

But God brought about something surprising and extraordinary.

Genevieve's dementia had progressed to the point where she had to live in a supervised apartment that provided meal services but no medical services. One day I received a phone call from a cook at the facility, informing me that Genevieve was acting strangely and appeared to have some paralysis on one side. I immediately left for the facility, where I found Genevieve lying on the bed with what appeared to be a significant impairment on her left side. I would have bet the farm that she had suffered a stroke.

Quickly I arranged to get her to the hospital and called her neurologist, asking her to meet us at the emergency room. After an initial examination, the neurologist also suspected a stroke and arranged to have blood tests done and scheduled an MRI. As Sharon and I described to Genevieve the implications of a stroke and how it would change the way we cared for her, the neurologist returned to the room with some test results.

"I'm afraid I was wrong," she said, waving the sheet in front of me. "Her blood alcohol level is high. She's drunk."

Her words hit me like cold drops of water in a hot skillet. I exploded. I screamed at my mother-in-law, "That's just *great*! Don't you realize how selfish you are? Don't you know how difficult you are? You have made my life miserable, when all we've tried to do is take care of you! You think the only thing we have to do is take care of you! Don't you realize how you're ruining my life?"

All those hateful words—and more—spewed from my mouth. I threw insults at a woman who, for the most part, had done nothing to me—a woman who had survived tragedy of the kind that would have sent most of us leaping off a bridge, a woman who had responded to her pain by forging ahead and making a good and wholesome life for her children.

Eventually Genevieve sobered up, and I took her home. She apologized, but I knew I had a much deeper apology to make.

It took this ugly incident to show me that in all my caregiving, I had yet to learn how to really love. I had gone through the motions of caregiving and even knew a lot about how to be helpful. But I saw myself as a hero to be admired and respected for all the sacrifices I had made. So when my caregiving was ineffective or thwarted and the problems refused to go away – when I received no pats on the back or rousing accolades – I became angry and depressed. That is what exploded out of me when Genevieve drank too much. I certainly was no hero.

I apologized to Genevieve because I realized that God had brought me to a place where I truly had to reckon with the issue of love – a love not predicated on recognition or response, but an unselfish and giving kind of love. God wasn't seeking to use me in Genevieve's life simply to give her care; he was seeking to use Genevieve in my life to make me more giving, caring, and genuinely loving. In short, God was using Genevieve (and her need to receive care) in order to mold and make me to be more like Jesus – the one who loves perfectly.

And so God used a frail old woman who suffered with Alzheimer's to change my life. He used her to get the point across that I was *not* some heroic, good man who gave unselfishly. I was a proud man who wanted things my way, a vain man who wanted to be recognized and praised. After that shattering moment when God confronted my character and caused me to face myself, I realized that God was asking me to become a humble servant who would be willing to love, no matter the response or outcome. He was asking me to become a sacrificial lover of my mother-in-law who would be willing to show her kindness for the rest of her days. He was asking me to understand the true application of my faith: "Religion that God our Father accepts as pure and faultless is this: to look after orphans and widows in their distress" (James 1:27).

God is asking the boomer generation to recognize something special in the process of caregiving. He is asking us to not only become the first Caregiving Generation due to sociological reasons but to become caregivers for the purpose of changing *us*.

We became famous in the 1960s, partly because we were part of the "peace and love" generation. We accepted the idea from humanistic psychology that unconditional positive regard, acceptance, and empathy were the only things necessary to bring about peace. Somehow, we began to equate God's *agapē* love with this unconditional acceptance. We thought it meant taking us and others exactly where we are, with no expectations.

But although this unconditional acceptance is part of *agapē* love, it certainly is not the most important aspect. *Agapē* love is truly altruistic and sacrificial. It not only gives out of an abundance of love; it is willing to give even when that love hurts. In other words, suppose we have one loaf of bread. We both stand at the edge of starvation, and we know that if we split the bread, both of us will die. *Agapē* love causes me to give you the bread and say, "Take and eat." The depth of *agapē* means I will give to you, even if it means my own demise.

Most of us are willing to have this kind of love for our children. Somehow it seems easier to love these rosy-cheeked gifts from God, so full of potential with nothing but growth and possibilities ahead of them. But it is a real challenge to give this kind of love to our elders. Give to elders who have all of their growth behind them? Give to cranky older people who decay and who are sliding inevitably toward death?

Yes. To love that which is most decayed—this is what loving and caregiving is all about.

But surely this is what *all of us* must look like to Christ! And yet he chose to love and die for us. And herein lies the potential: if we can learn to truly love our aging parents in such an unselfish and sacrificial way, then we will be learning to be more like Christ.

Our elders have the power to change our characters and our personhoods. It is what Chris de Vinck calls "the power of the powerless."* Our aging parents are frail and needy, and they see their lives quickly disappearing. Nevertheless, these elders have the power to give us the opportunity to learn one of the greatest lessons of giving and growing in Christ.

Becoming the Caregiving Generation will cost us dearly. Our friendships will have to be placed on the back burner, our financial portfolios will likely deteriorate, and many of our relationships will decline. But there is a gift here in becoming the Caregiving Generation—the gift of truly knowing how to love like Christ. Love does not teach us much when life is easy; love teaches us everything when life is hard and costs the lover much.

Genevieve passed in the winter of 2006. Did I learn to love her perfectly? Certainly not. But I did learn to love her better and more sacrificially than I ever thought I could. If you are willing to learn, then this caregiving opportunity that has come to you (or will soon come) can bring out more love in you than you ever thought possible.

---

* See Christopher de Vinck, *The Power of the Powerless* (Grand Rapids: Zondervan, 1995).

2

THE BIG THREE TRANSITIONS:
HOUSE, MONEY, AND CAR

I live in the part of the country known as "Tornado Alley." Every spring, when the weather starts to warm up, several afternoons will see the right combinations of air mass and moisture to fire up severe thunderstorms. And with these thunderstorms — some of which can grow to unbelievable intensity — comes the inevitable wind, lightning, hail, and tornadoes that cause devastation.

Where we live, it's not a matter of *if* this kind of weather is going to hit but of *where* and *when*. Each year, hail and wind cause terrific damage in our area, and at least a couple of nearby towns have endured the ravages of a tornado.

As a result, people in this region have a plan for severe weather. We have a closet in an interior hall that is well protected and located away from windows. Although a tornado has never hit our town directly, we have spent many hours in the hall, ready to dive into the closet at a moment's notice.

Boomers in the twenty-first century live in "Caregiving Alley." For most of us, it's not a matter of *if* we will have an aging parent who will need our caregiving but *where* and *when*. As a result, we must have a plan in place that can be executed quickly and efficiently.

Perhaps there was a time when we could just hope that our parents wouldn't require care, but in sociological terms, that time has long since passed. Well over two-thirds of boomers will have to give some type of care to an aging parent. If you choose to wait to make your plan until your elder parent needs assistance, you'll likely end up flirting with disaster. Suppose you know that your elderly parent needs to have his or her home modified or needs to move to a simpler and safer living situation; suppose it's long past the time when he or she should stop driving. If you wait until your parent falls and breaks a hip or crashes into a house before you take action, then rest assured that you will be playing catch-up with a much more complicated caregiving situation. It would be a little like seeking shelter after a tornado has already hit.

If you are going to live responsibly in this age and time, it is wise to assume you will be caring for an aging parent—and therefore it's best to get ready, make plans early, and execute these plans before the tornado of aging hits!

The Myth of Role Reversal

It is important to remember that caregiving is primarily about a *relationship*. You don't get to make all the decisions in a vacuum and then execute the plan under martial law. You are connected to your aging parent, who is fully vested in his or her adulthood. Unless you are willing to jump over all of the legal hurdles involved in getting your aging parent declared "incompetent" and having the court appoint you as legal guardian (a tedious and often difficult process), the elder is guaranteed by law to have exactly the same rights and privileges as you. Therefore, it really is to your advantage that you and your aging parent learn how to work together constructively in the process of caregiving.

One thing that consistently works against this process of working together is the myth that caregivers have *switched roles* with their parents. The reasoning goes that, just as the parent once gave nurture and care to the child, so the aging parent is now in need of similar nurture and care from the adult child. This myth often leads well-meaning caregivers to see their aging parents as children who have little reasoning ability and who essentially cannot take care of anything themselves.

"But that's exactly how my parent acts!" some caregivers respond. "They do crazy things without explanation. They throw tantrums that aren't connected at all to reality. They can no longer manage any aspect of their life." All of these things may be true—but it still doesn't mean your parent has become your child.

The truth is that in your caregiving you may perform many of the activities common to childhood or infancy. You may manage their money, decide what they eat, help them get dressed, or even change their adult diapers. But even so, you will never be able to give to your parent what he or she gave to you. Parents have the original programming opportunity to teach their children about who they are and how to behave in relationships. Parents have the power to teach children that they are worthy, precious, desirable in relationship, and capable of responsible giving. In short, parents have an enormous effect on the original programming of a child's personality, self-image, and future trustworthiness. This opportunity belongs to the parent alone and is by far the most important duty of a parent.

When a well-meaning caregiver treats his or her aging parent as a child, the aging parent feels this sense of personhood violated. Would you not feel patronized if an adult treated you as though you no longer had the rights and privileges appropriate to your age? So it is that your adult parents feel patronized and dehumanized when you treat them like children. I may need you to feed and clothe me and even take care of my basic hygiene needs. But if you treat me like a child, I will feel insulted. And if I feel insulted, I will often respond in anger, defensiveness, and resentment, and I'll initiate a power struggle.

I became keenly aware of this fact when I served as a director of a personal care facility several years ago. The facility cared for moderately to severely affected Alzheimer's patients, and even when the older person could barely speak—and long past the time when he or she remembered his or her own name—staff members were urged to treat the individual as an adult. I remember the time when I informed Laura that she was about to get a shower, I caught myself talking to her in much the same tone and inflection I'd use with a three-year-old. Laura became extremely resistant and uncooperative. When I tried to insist on the shower, we became locked in a power struggle. Since Laura was in the moderate stages of Alzheimer's, I knew that the next day she'd be unlikely to remember either me or the conflict, and so I'd have a chance at a "do over."

The next time I came into her room, I said in my best "adult" voice, "Laura, today is the day we normally do showers. I know it's not something you want to do, but it is something that we have to do today if it's going to get done. Can you help me get this done?" I went to the bathroom and turned on the shower, assisted by one of the personal care aides. Within minutes, Laura shuffled into the bathroom and cooperated with the whole process.

Does this work every time? No, but it certainly has more success than locking into an insulting power struggle over whether the elder has the right to cooperate with his or her own care.

An aging parent may be cognitively, emotionally, and physically impaired, but he or she is still fully an adult. This truth is consistently reflected in the Bible. On their deathbeds, Abraham, Isaac, and David were deteriorating; yet the people around them treated them with respect and high regard, honoring their status of adulthood. When we see our aging parents as children, we strike a blow deep into their emotional cores. That emotional core is accustomed to being treated as an adult, and we will stir resentment if we insist on acting as though we are dealing with a child.

Examples from the Bible also suggest that the parent still holds the emotional and positional authority to "bless." Listen to the writer of Hebrews: "By faith Jacob, when he was dying, blessed each of Joseph's sons, and worshiped as he leaned on the top of his staff" (11:21). The implication is that the parent, no matter how old or impaired, has something we need.

I believe we need our parent's wisdom and knowledge, and their instilling of confidence in us that we ourselves are fully adult. In other words, no parent ever ceases to be a parent. These biblical examples indicate that our parents still have important things to teach us about life, relationships, and especially the process of dying. I'm convinced this is true even when the aging parent has a profound impairment.

I recall one elderly lady in the late stages of Alzheimer's who had lost her language skills. It was the Christmas season, and her daughter had come for a visit. During a small celebration in the dining room, the sounds of "Silent Night" filled the air. The daughter began to weep, because it was her mother's favorite carol, and she knew this was probably her mom's last Christmas on earth. As this elderly woman became aware of her daughter's weeping, she placed her hand on her daughter's hand and sang a verse of "Silent Night" — even though she hadn't spoken in months and had very little cognitive awareness. She was obviously trying to tell the daughter something very deep indeed. I believe she was moving around the thick curtain of dementia to give her daughter one last parental gift.

Even until the very end, our parents remain our parents. They will never become our children. At the same time, we are not children anymore. We are adults charged with the responsibility of caring for our parents and reckoning with the reality of their limitations. We cannot order what is best for them in terms of taking a parental position, but we can move into a position of cooperation with them to negotiate some of the tough terrain of aging and some of the practical issues, such as housing, finances, and driving.

Keep in mind that we cannot dictate to our parents the caregiving plan. As I said in the introduction, most of our parents come from what has been called "the greatest generation" — a generation who grew up in the midst of the Great Depression and answered the call in the desperate times of World War II and the Korean War. As a group, they are "tough old birds" who know how to weather the storms of life, make necessary sacrifices, and survive whatever life tosses at them. Most never considered the possibility they would ever need to receive care. They believed they would care for themselves, with tenacity and independence, and would die in their sleep. But the sea change in medicine and health care makes that, at least for the majority of this "greatest generation," highly unlikely. How do we give care to such an independent group of people who will likely resist our efforts?

The big thing to remember is to *talk early and talk often*. Our parents come from a generation of strong and tough-minded people. Nevertheless, we boomers are practiced and persistent in knowing how to bring about change. Part of the secret to bringing about cooperative change with our parents is to bring up the key subjects — things such as housing, finances, and driving

— *before* the need arises to move, give up control, or hand over the keys.

Begin with conversations that include questions such as, "What circumstances could happen that would cause you to move? How would you like me to handle your finances or estate if a time comes when you cannot manage them yourself or when you die? Have you thought about what you will do if you can no longer drive?" These starter questions often get shrugged off initially with one- or two-word answers. But this is where the strength of the boomer generation lies: we are a persistent bunch. Perhaps at first you'll let a short answer stand, but if you keep bringing up the subject every few weeks and ask for more conversation, eventually you'll prompt a fuller conversation. These conversations, in turn, will form the basis for the cooperative effort that in time will coalesce into a plan. *Talk early and talk often*—this should become the battle cry for boomer caregivers.

Certainly the issues of caregiving and methods of completing the job are as varied as there are individual situations. But in my experience, most caregivers have to address three major issues in the job of caregiving—housing, finances, and driving. To these I'll now turn.

The Challenge of Housing

One factor, above all others, gives older adults the highest life satisfaction, namely, *independence.* They want the independence and freedom to control their relationships, finances, health issues, and housing choices. And home—whether a house, condo, or apartment—is a particularly powerful predictor of whether the older adult feels independent.

As your parent grows elderly, most of his or her friends will die or move. He or she may lose the cognitive ability to manage his or her own money. And the decline of life will likely mean that he or she will be in poor to fair health. All of these losses of independence make it even more predictable that the older parent will hang on to his or her home as the last bastion of independence. These realities will make the transition a bit trickier but certainly not impossible to negotiate. The first step in determining which type of housing situation is best for your parent is to assess his or her physical capabilities.

Making Sense of Physical Decline

Not all physical impairment is equal. Some older people have problems such as arthritis that can be debilitating and demand intense physical assistance, while others have serious ailments such as diabetes that still allow them to keep their own garden or go for daily walks. It takes clear thinking and careful communication in order to accurately assess the physical capabilities and limitations of your older parent.

People who work in elder care use several tools to help assess how much or how little an older person can take care of himself or herself. One such tool is called Instrumental Activities of Daily Living—IADLs for short. These IADLs look at several activities required to maintain independent living, such as carrying out housekeeping tasks, doing laundry, cooking meals, driving, planning, paying bills, and knowing how, when, and what medications are to be taken. Another tool is called Activities of Daily Living, or ADLs. The ADLs involve issues of *independent function* and include things such as the ability to eat without assistance, bathing, dressing, toileting, basic hygiene such as brushing teeth, and getting up and around.

We use IADLs and ADLs to determine what kind of physical limitations an older person has. Most often, there will be a predictable deterioration with IADLs before there is deterioration in ADLs. For instance, you are likely to see a decline first in your parent's ability to shop, cook meals, clean the home, and do the laundry (IADLs). As aging and decline persists, you will then likely see a decline in his or her ability to perform basic hygiene, such as bathing or brushing teeth, dressing himself or herself, or being able to manage his or her own toileting needs (ADLs). Unless some accident or sudden illness occurs, such as a fractured hip or stroke, you will almost always be able to count on this predictable pattern.

We knew that my mother-in-law was cognitively deteriorating. We first began to see that she was having difficulty cooking meals, and when she did cook, the menu items didn't make much sense. She began to avoid driving or going out to purchase basic necessities. Soon she had stopped cleaning her apartment altogether. Certainly she was able to feed herself, get dressed independently, and had no trouble with mobility, but even so, she needed assistance with the Instrumental Activities of Daily Living. We would clean her apartment for her, and Sharon would do the shopping. We tried to cook some meals for her and have Meals on Wheels delivered to her home. None of this initial care demanded that she make a move from her apartment, where she had lived for years.

A mild stroke compelled Genevieve to have to spend several days at the hospital. When she returned home, it soon became evident that she had stopped bathing herself and was neglecting her teeth. She also began to have difficulty recognizing people and couldn't remember the correct day of the week. Soon it became clear that both her IADLs and her ADLs had deteriorated to the point where she could no longer live by herself. So we initiated a move to an apartment complex where she could get meal service. As the Alzheimer's caused greater and greater dementia, she needed caregiving help to take care of not only all of her IADLs — such as finances, shopping, medications, and laundry—but eventually all of her ADLs as well, such as bathing, dressing, feeding, and taking medications.

To accurately assess Genevieve's housing needs, we had to first assess her ability to live independently and take care of herself. A simplified checklist of IADLs and ADLs is provided on page 77 to help you in assessing your aging parent's ability to maintain independent living.

After determining the physical capability of your elder, it is necessary to know the options for housing and have some basis on which to make a decision about the best fit for the parent.

Knowing the Housing Options

The best housing option for an older person is to stay in his or her home if at all possible. But realize that most homes or apartments are not built with elders in mind. When an elder has difficulty with orientation, mobility, or eyesight, the home once considered a safe haven might turn into an obstacle course. Still, if possible, it is reasonable to make either physical or service modifications to the home in order to help the older person stay put.

More injuries occur in the bathroom than anywhere else in the home. There you find combinations of twisting, turning, bending, reaching, and stepping over, done mostly in the presence of water on tile and bare feet. A few commonsense modifications can make all the difference in the world. For instance, install handrails around the toilet, tub, and shower. In addition, replace the toilet with a taller model or put on a raised seat. Using a bath chair in the tub or shower makes getting in and out much easier. In most cases, showers are much safer than tubs because of the big step required to get into a tub.

Think also about where water can accumulate and where bending and stepping take place. At these places, slips can quickly turn into falls, which often can result in broken bones.

IADLs and ADLs
Assessment Guide

Area	Function or Task	Can perform task reasonably well	Has difficulty performing task regularly	Caregiving required to accomplish task
Nutrition				
IADLs	Planning appropriate meals	☐	☐	☐
	Cooking meals safely	☐	☐	☐
ADLs	Knowing when to eat	☐	☐	☐
	Feeding oneself	☐	☐	☐
Mobility				
IADLs	Driving oneself or taking a bus	☐	☐	☐
	Doing grocery shopping	☐	☐	☐
	Running errands	☐	☐	☐
ADLs	Walking without assistance	☐	☐	☐
	Transferring from chairs or bed without assistance	☐	☐	☐
Medications				
IADLs	Knowing medication regimen	☐	☐	☐
	Reordering medications	☐	☐	☐
ADLs	Taking medications unassisted	☐	☐	☐
Managing				
IADLs	Doing unassisted housekeeping	☐	☐	☐
	Managing finances	☐	☐	☐
	Using telephone	☐	☐	☐
ADLs	Being oriented to time/place	☐	☐	☐
	Behaving appropriately in social situations	☐	☐	☐
Hygiene				
IADLs	Taking care of laundry	☐	☐	☐
ADLs	Bathing/showering	☐	☐	☐
	Toileting without assistance	☐	☐	☐
	Dressing oneself	☐	☐	☐
	Brushing teeth	☐	☐	☐

Nonskid mats or stickers are helpful in areas where stepping down frequently takes place. Try to minimize uneven surfaces that invite trips or stumbles. Replace the showerhead with a handheld shower nozzle.

The next most threatening area for older people is the kitchen. Here, too, the injuries come primarily from falling because of so many opportunities for bending and twisting. Modifications to cabinets are essential. Most elders will need only a few items from their cabinets; it should be easy to place essential items in the lower shelves for easy reach. Extra pots and pans must be removed and stored. If these items remain, the elder will often go looking for something and will use a stool or chair to open the cabinet door. If necessary, remove the cabinet doors so he or she can see that the shelves are bare.

You may want to change the dials on the kitchen stove to ones that have large labels. Keep only the appliances that the elder is able to use effectively, since doing so greatly decreases the risk of leaving something on or accidentally turning on an appliance. Automatic shutoffs are always a plus. Replace breakable dishes with unbreakable ones to reduce the risk of cuts.

Make sure the rest of the house has secure handrails around any steps, and take care to assure that all carpets and rugs are flat and secure. Removing unused furniture such as tables, lamps, and chairs makes walking through the house much easier. Lift chairs or straight-back chairs are much easier for the older person to use when getting up and down. Remember that aesthetics are not the main objective when your loved one wants to stay at home. Offering a safe environment must be the top priority.

One of the most significant things you can do to modify the physical space of a home is to limit the usable space. A home becomes far safer for an elder if the upstairs and basement are permanently blocked off. Also, consider using rooms for purposes other than their original intended use. For instance, sometimes the dining room can be used as a bedroom. This arrangement can connect three rooms—living room, dining room (now the bedroom), and kitchen—into a very effective efficiency apartment. Not only does the living space become much safer; it also relieves the elder of the worries of trying to take care of the rest of the house. Modifications such as these can often remove the need for your loved one to move into a care facility and will usually result in the older parent being much happier.

Another way to keep an elder at home is to make service modifications intended to help the older person take their medications, cook meals, or receive some type of health service. A wide range of service modifications are available. Sometimes the only service modification required is a meal service that will provide regular nutrition, such as Meals on Wheels.

Most often, however, the type of service required will increase as the older parent becomes frailer. Two common options include a home personal care worker and a home health aide. Home personal care workers usually work for an agency and are trained to assist older people with household and personal hygiene tasks. These workers can usually be scheduled for particular days or hours. Many elders can function well at home if they have regular assistance to get over the rough spots in the day such as bathing, getting up in the morning, and doing some housecleaning.

Home health aides function more like nursing assistants and also usually work through agencies. These employees provide professional medical assistance. Most times, health aides can perform the necessary health service at a lower cost; but if nursing care is required, most agencies that provide health aides also can provide registered nurses who make home visits. Remember, however, that nursing care services provided several hours every day can equal the cost of residence in an assisted living facility.

Be cautious if you consider hiring individuals not referred by health care agencies. These individuals often aren't specifically trained to work with elders and can lack the skills to do an effective job. But an even greater concern is the risk of exposing your loved one to unscrupulous or dishonest individuals. Many independents who work in the caregiving field are wonderful, nurturing people, but sadly, a growing number of predators are offering their "services" in the field of caregiving. Many are simply thieves who intend to steal valuables from your older parent's home. Others work to win the affections of you and your elder in order to gain power over your loved one's finances, either through placing an extra name on an account or, even worse, to gain the power of attorney. Others will work to gain access to records, credit cards, and financial accounts and steal the elder's identity or defraud accounts. Unfortunately, the stories of people being taken in by these kinds of scam artists are legion.

If you choose to hire an independent worker, recognize that the person will not *look* like a scam artist. He or she will look and act totally trustworthy. Ask for references (and call them!) and carefully check out past work situations. Besides simply calling the references, ask for the names and numbers of other relatives as well; then call and talk to them. If such names and numbers cannot be provided, then you should probably take a pass on the individual. Elders living at home are easy targets, so take extreme care to make sure they are protected. Your local Area Agency on Aging (AAA) should have a list of reputable service providers in your area.

When a Move Is Necessary

Whether an older parent's home becomes unsafe or he or she has ailments that demand comprehensive health care, it may become necessary at some point to make a move. The first question caregivers often ask is whether they should move their loved ones into their own homes.

Full-time caregiving under your own roof can be highly challenging but also rewarding, for you, your elder, and your family. But you should go into this type of situation with eyes wide open. Be completely honest about your schedule, your energy, and the desires and needs of other people in your household.

First, take a look at your house. Is your house safer than the home of your aging parent? If it's less safe, are you willing and able to make the necessary modifications? Understand that modifications will likely make your home feel less "homey." You may not think it's a big deal to modify the family den in order to accommodate an additional bedroom, but what do other family members think? They may have strong feelings on the matter. Take care to seek agreement from the entire family about adding another family member to the home.

Also ask yourself hard questions about whether you have the necessary skills to care for your aging parent. Sometimes these skills can be learned, and sometimes they can be provided by a health care agency, but be realistic in assessing the care you can provide.

Finally, be honest with yourself and your family regarding the emotional wear and tear that caring for an older parent will bring. Even in the best of situations, the day-in and day-out nature of providing care can cause great stress. And in difficult situations, caregiving may require more emotional energy than you possess.

If you feel up to the task of caregiving under your own roof, remember to take advantage of services often provided in metropolitan communities, which can include senior citizen centers, adult day care agencies, and transportation help. These services can often provide you with or link you to emotional support with other caregivers, as well as providing necessary and much needed respite.

Caregiving in your home can offer an intimacy with your aging parent that provides a setting for meaningful connection as well as an opportunity to teach the family firsthand about aging and giving. While live-in caregiving does involve inconvenience and sacrifice, the resulting connection between family members is often exactly what is wanted and needed.

If you cannot give your loved one care in your own home, don't feel guilty. Sometimes memories of an old television show like *The Waltons* from the 1970s can give us a warm glow about caregiving for an elder. We imagine an intergenerational family all pulling together as one and becoming very close.

Recognize first of all that this picture has little to do with the reality of our past (or even other cultures' pasts). Very few households have *ever* been caregiving places for elders. What's more, the world has changed significantly in the last fifty years. Long gone are the days where we could count on at least one spouse in a family being at home. This makes full-time caregiving for an aging parent almost impossible. Finally, decisions made out of guilt often lead to regret. If you want caring for an aging parent in the home to be a connecting growth opportunity, then your heart must clearly say yes to it. If guilt prompts you to provide care inside your home, then at best you will come to resent your loved one, and at worst you may become deeply depressed.

The care industry offers good options for elders. Many unlicensed facilities offer efficiency apartments or houses while providing some type of service opportunities. These facilities are often connected to retirement homes or elder communities that have a wide variety of living spaces and offer immediate access to daily meals, housekeeping services, and medical facilities. The prices on these facilities are usually quite reasonable, but typically they offer no hygiene assistance, no medication monitoring, and little health care. In these types of facilities, the elder is expected to maintain independent living while taking advantage of the on-campus services. The key word is *services,* not *care,* so it's clearly not appropriate for all aging parents.

The next level of care is a licensed residence called a personal care home or personal assistance facility. These facilities are inspected at regular intervals; reports on these inspections should be readily available for your investigation. Usually these facilities have one- or two-room apartments clustered under one roof. The services provided by these facilities vary for particular residents, but usually they have twenty-four-hour supervision, nursing care, bathing and grooming assistance, housekeeping and laundry services, ambulation assistance, medication monitoring, transportation services, and social activities. Often such facilities have three levels of care. Each level provides more services at a greater total cost. Usually the older person has an initial evaluation to determine an appropriate level of care, followed by evaluations every few months to determine if any change has occurred.

These facilities provide all of the care of what used to be called nursing homes, with the exception of medical assistance. Even though staff members provide medication monitoring (ordering and supervising the taking of medications), they cannot administer the medications themselves; nor can they render medical assistance, except in case of an emergency. But clearly these facilities fill the gap by providing residents with much of their required daily assistance, while also giving much needed supervision and ensuring safety. They also allow residents to maintain a level of independence.

When your parent needs constant medical care, the best option may be a nursing care facility. Nursing facilities provide similar services to those provided by personal care facilities,

with the addition of medical professionals who can administer and render medical aid. Most of these facilities have either
private or semiprivate rooms and require residents to sleep in
a hospital bed. The facility will have full-time nursing staff as
well as health care aides. In general, nursing care facilities have
many of the same amenities as personal care facilities but not
as much personal room for residents or as many opportunities
for independence.

As you carefully consider the type of facility to choose, remember to look ahead and determine if the facility can provide
care for your loved one for a reasonable length of time, given
your parent's rate of decline. If your aging parent is on the edge
of being too infirm for the level of care the facility provides, it
may be best to opt for the next level of care. On the other hand,
pay close attention to the services your parent will actually need.
If he or she will use only one or two services, it might be best to
choose a lower level of care. Also investigate whether the facility has a good reputation. If it is licensed, inspect the reports for
the past several years. Check with your local Area Agency on
Aging and the state's regulatory system to make sure the facility
has a good record. Be willing to talk with residents and families
of residents to get their impressions of care and satisfaction. And
finally, don't hesitate to drop in on the facility when no one is
expecting you. You should be seeing the same level of attention
and care when you drop in as when you are expected.

Once you determine the level of care and living situation best
suited for your aging parent, you can begin to work with him
or her in making the transition. It's usually best to start these
discussions early and talk often about the options. But once
the decision is made, exercise care in helping the elder "close
down" his or her home. I often recommend that the caregiver
and parent go through the house and thoughtfully determine
who should get certain treasured items. This intentionality of

giving away the "stuff" of the elder may provoke sadness, but in the long run it helps him or her deal with the grief associated with the move. Also, I often recommend a ceremonial closing of the home once the aging parent is ready to move. Frequently this means one last family dinner in which family members sit down together to eat and to reflect on the memories generated in that home. While this too may spur sadness, in the long run it assists the elder in dealing with the long-term effects of grieving the loss of the home.

The Challenge of Money

Although many of our aging parents have profound physical ailments that require intense and full-time care, their minds often remain as sharp as tacks! In such cases, it is not unusual for them to maintain control of their finances right up until the moment of death.

If this describes your parent, the situation may frustrate you at times because it tends to prompt more problems associated with negotiation and payment for care – but realize that it truly is a blessing. Caregivers who must take control of a parent's finances usually are dealing with dementia, Alzheimer's disease, or a parent's inability to cognitively function due to injury or illness. And this is the reality many of us will face! Few aging parents will suffer from significant dementia before the age of eighty, but after the age of eighty-five, nearly one in every two older persons has some form of dementia. This fact makes the prospect of managing an aging parent's finances quite high.

Let me be clear, however: if you are a caregiver – or likely to become one – it is *your* responsibility to broach the subject of finances with your loved one. It is your business because, at the minimum, you are going to be heavily involved in making the decisions concerning the care of the elder, and costs and resources must be figured into the consideration. At the maximum, you may eventually be responsible for administering the finances. It is reasonable that your aging parent remains in control of his or her finances for as long as possible. But it is wise to be aware of his or her financial situation if you will become the one responsible for caregiving.

Taking Stock and Making a Plan

Negotiating this transition first has to do with awareness. Here too, talk early and talk often. Ask such questions as, "Mom, I need to know some of the specifics of your finances in case I ever become responsible for you," or "Dad, if you begin to need care and can't make your own decisions, how do you want me to manage your money?" These kinds of questions open the door for more specific investigations of finances.

Remember that your aging parent may initially resist the idea of "opening the books," but your persistence will eventually result in gaining more information, which will allow you to form a good idea of the financial picture.

Nevertheless, the topic of finances is a difficult one to bring up. We worry that our aging parents will suspect us of being interested only in their money. Most caregivers have absolutely pure motives in asking for this information, but it is wise to check your motives and make sure your interest in their finances is wholesome. It amazes me to find that more and more boomers worry about how much money will be left in the estate after a parent's death instead of being concerned about how that money can effectively be used for the parent's care. While it is reasonable for the caregiver to wish to receive some of the estate, at best it must be a secondary priority.

As you seek to understand your aging parent's finances, it is wise to include siblings, financial advisers, a lawyer, or another family member to serve as a check to make sure your motives are clean. If you are unwilling to involve one of these people, it may be a sign that you are no longer acting in your parent's best interest.

After you gain awareness of the financial picture, it is necessary to determine a plan with regard to what your parent will need for care and how much control you will eventually need to take. I suggest that caregivers think through three scenarios:

- the parent stays in his or her current condition and can manage resources by himself or herself

- the parent worsens substantially and needs a progression of care, which dictates substantial assistance in managing resources

- the parent becomes totally incapacitated and cannot make independent decisions, requiring the caregiver to make all financial decisions

Of course, we hope for the best situation, but we need to be prepared for the worst. In each scenario, it is essential to determine the resources available to your parent. First, take into account any monthly income coming from Social Security, pensions, or investment income. Then include the principal of any resources such as stocks, bonds, 401(k) accounts, individual retirement accounts (IRAs), certificates of deposit (CDs), real estate, and cash accounts. With this total asset picture, you can start looking realistically at the costs for each of the three scenarios — costs that will vary greatly.

If your parent stays in his or her current condition, he or she may do quite well on his or her present income without ever touching the principal in investments. If he or she worsens and requires significant assistance or medical attention, meeting these needs may well increase expenses by $1,000 to $3,000 a month. If your parent becomes incapacitated and needs full-time care and medical assistance, expenses could well go up by $3,000 to $6,000 a month.

Depending on the principal resources that are over and above the income your parent receives, it's easy to see how his or her care needs could exhaust resources within a relatively short period of time. Therefore, it is wise to anticipate the various scenarios so that you can envision the kind of care that can be paid for out of your parent's resources, where he or she may eventually need help from the family or need to go on government assistance.

Paying for Medical Assistance

One of the huge issues caregivers must deal with is how to pay for and manage health care. Fortunately, Medicare provides some medical assistance to older people.

Medicare

Medicare is a federal government insurance program currently available to people aged sixty-five and older, although the parent must apply for and receive a Medicare card. The plan consists of four parts:

- One part of Medicare covers most of the costs associated with hospital stays and bills. Like any insurance program, this part has premiums to pay and deductibles to be met.

- A second part of Medicare covers expenses incurred from doctors, laboratories, outpatient services, and supplies. This part also has required premiums and deductibles but pays only a percentage of the care and services provided. Most often, your parent is responsible for 20 percent of the cost associated with this part.

Because these deductibles and percentage costs can be quite high, many people choose to pay for a "medigap" policy. This separate insurance policy pays, in varying degrees depending on cost, the "gap" of expenses that normally would fall to your parent. The federal government and Medicare maintain a list of reputable companies that offer these kinds of policies, so investigate carefully before you make a purchase.

- A third part of Medicare provides a prescription drug benefit. The program essentially requires enrollment in a specific subprogram that provides coverage for certain medications only. Your parent would enroll in the subprogram best suited for the medications he or she uses. This relatively new program has confused many recipients and has offered varying degrees of benefit.

  Although these three parts of Medicare have some negative aspects, their benefits are undeniable. Unless your parent has another medical insurance plan as part of a retirement package, Medicare likely will cover him or her.

- A fourth part of Medicare provides an option to join a managed care organization, or HMO; in this case, the HMO receives a fee from the government. Participation depends on whether the older person lives in an area where there is a managed care organization that offers this option. The plan essentially includes the first two parts of Medicare outlined above. The HMO offers set guidelines and an approved network of providers for its enrollees.

If you are the caregiver for your aging parent, most likely you will have to be heavily involved with his or her health care insurance. Inevitably, disputes will arise about payments and services. You must be willing to deal with these disputes and help your parent resolve the issues in order to protect your parent's resources.

Medicaid

Medicaid is a government insurance program designed to benefit people who live in poverty. Although the federal government pays for the program, it is administered by each state. If your older parent lives below the poverty line, he or she likely will qualify for Medicaid. Generally, if your elder is covered by Medicaid, he or she is not required to pay premiums or meet deductibles. In addition, Medicaid covers hospital stays, doctor visits, and all prescriptions. Unlike Medicare, Medicaid provides payment for long-term care facilities.

In order to qualify for Medicaid, however, your aging parent essentially must have extinguished *all* of his or her existing resources, including real estate, personal belongings, household goods, cash value of insurance policies, and any investments. You cannot legally move any of these resources into your name or another person's name and expect your parent to qualify for Medicaid. Medicaid is meant for the truly poverty-stricken, not for those wishing to preserve resources of an estate.

The Power to Make Financial Decisions

As I observed earlier, I believe the best model for caregiving involves one primary caregiver and one primary caregiver support group. In order to be an effective caregiver, you need the legal and financial power to work in concert with the level of responsibility you undertake.

Be clear on this: you do not have authority to dictate terms. Instead of being *authoritarian*, think in terms of being *authoritative*. Authoritarian people are rigid and demand that things conform exactly to their stated wishes. They invite little or no communication about decision making; they simply want to enforce their decisions. Authoritative people, on the other hand, are clearly leaders who invite and accept input from all who have an interest in the situation — the aging parent, family members, friends, and siblings. An authoritative caregiver makes decisions only after thoughtfully considering everyone's ideas and input. Certainly, an authoritative person is in control and in power, but the way he or she makes and implements decisions looks very different from the way an authoritarian personality does it. While I believe that caregivers need the power and authority to execute good decision making, it's always best to come to these decisions with the benefit of wise counsel, open communication, and input from all parties interested in the situation.

A caregiver essentially needs to be given power to make decisions regarding financial, health care, and living situations. While a caregiver can exercise some financial control by doing simple things — such as having a checking account with the elder in which the caregiver has authority to sign checks — when it comes to making complex decisions, it is usually necessary to have some legal mechanism in place.

The first legal mechanism is called *guardianship*. In guardianship, a court must decree that your older parent is incompetent or unable to carry out his or her affairs. Although state laws vary, typically the court authorizes someone to manage all of the older person's affairs, just as if the older person had no decision-making ability. While this may sound like a dramatic step, sometimes mental or physical deterioration takes place before arrangements can be made. Without the older person's consent (given in a mentally sound state of mind), a caregiver may be forced to pursue this avenue in order to get the authority to make business, financial, and health care decisions. Guardianship is complicated, and it is necessary to have an attorney to draft a petition to the court. If you are appointed as guardian of your parent, then you have total legal responsibility for the elder—and no one can relieve you of that obligation except the court.

A much easier option is that of *power of attorney*. Here the caregiver is given the authority to do business on behalf of the parent that includes handling banking needs, overseeing financial accounts, buying or selling real estate, and purchasing or selling stocks and bonds. It is wise to have this document drawn up by an attorney to ensure that it is correct and that both you and your parent are well informed with regard to its powers and limitations. There are three types of power of attorney:

- general power of attorney, which gives you the right to act for a specific period of time on certain issues

- trigger power of attorney, which allows you to act once some type of "trigger" occurs, such as a hospitalization or diagnosis of Alzheimer's

- durable power of attorney, which allows you to act on all business items for an indefinite period

No matter what type of power of attorney you and your parent choose to employ, it does not forbid your parent from doing business on his or her own behalf. Therefore, it is very important for caregiver and elder to keep in close communication with regard to any business involving the older parent.

While the power of attorney allows the caregiver to do business in the name of the older parent, it does not give any authority with regard to health care decisions. Although it is wise for an elder to have a living will—which indicates the kind of medical interventions and treatments he or she wants or doesn't want in the event of terminal illness, injury, or incapacitation and inability to make decisions—I think such a living will is inadequate to ensure that the wishes of the elder are carried out. So I also recommend that the elder give the caregiver a *durable health care power of attorney* or *health care proxy*. These instruments are legally executed documents, just like a regular power of attorney, which give the caregiver the ability to make health care decisions if the older parent becomes incapacitated. These documents can contain very specific directions, and the elder and caregiver can work together to ensure that the types of treatment, conditions that enable decision making, and desires concerning treatment are explicitly stated.

The Challenge of Driving

The ability to drive is perhaps second only to the ability to continue living in one's home in terms of maintaining a sense of independence. In general, we North Americans love our cars and regard them as essential for going where we want to go and doing what we want to do. This attitude is no different for older persons. In many cases, driving is essential for them to maintain independence. So it is no surprise that as an older person starts his or her decline, driving is a very tough thing to give up and thus a difficult transition for the caregiver to encourage.

When should an elder hand over the keys? It is difficult to make a hard-and-fast rule because each situation is different. Generally, the caregiver should look for a decline in hand-eye coordination, slowing reaction times, poor depth perception, declining vision, and problems in general awareness. But remember that older people often learn how to compensate adequately for these problems.

It is common for family members to demand that their older parents stop driving when they no longer drive like everyone else does. But their driving habits may be a far cry from being unsafe. I often ask the caregiver to ride along with the loved one to the store or other destination. I'll then ask the caregiver, "Even though your older parent drives differently from the way you do, did he or she do anything unsafe?" Many times the elder will drive more slowly, wait longer at intersections, or hesitate in accelerating, but he or she will not do anything unsafe. In many cases, their driving habits are merely reflecting the kinds of things older people do to compensate for their slower reactions. It's how they make sure things remain safe.

Where necessary, however, you may be able to modify the driving habits of the older person. Perhaps you can negotiate a plan that would keep your loved one from driving on expressways or busy streets. Many older people can easily navigate to a pharmacy on an uncrowded street, for example. Getting your loved one accustomed to having you share his or her driving can be an important intermediate step to some day giving up driving totally.

But even after certain modifications and steps have been implemented, the elder may reach the point where he or she has no business driving any longer and yet refuses to give up the keys. In these cases, it's usually helpful to get an outside opinion. Work with the older parent to be evaluated by your state's appropriate agency (Department of Motor Vehicles, Secretary of State, Department of Public Safety, and so forth) to see if he or she can pass a normal driving test. In most states, you can let this agency know of your suspicions that your older parent may no longer be safe on the road. The agency can then request that he or she come in for a driving exam.

Another option is to ensure that the elder has adequate access to transportation. Metropolitan areas often have good access to public transportation and taxis. Many communities provide subsidized, low-cost transportation services for seniors. But if you live in a place where these options are not available, you may have to arrange to either drive the older person yourself or have someone else drive him or her. This can be time-consuming and expensive, but it is very difficult for older persons to conceptualize how to give up driving if you provide no options for getting out to the store, going to appointments, or socializing with friends.

In the end, you must use sober judgment with regard to your older parent driving. If he or she becomes a menace, you must take steps to protect both your parent and others. It may mean you must insist and not give up; it may mean you must leave with car keys in hand. Just as "friends don't let friends drink and drive," so also "caregivers don't let impaired elders drive." Don't wait until a serious accident occurs in which someone is injured or killed. You know what needs to be done, so take action *now*.

3

THE THREE "DS":
DEPRESSION, DEMENTIA, AND DEATH

Caregiving *will* change your life. It will change the way you go about your daily routines as you consider how to fulfill your obligations to your aging parent. It will change the amount of control you have over your own life and the way you exercise your freedom to go on vacation, take a short trip, or even enjoy a night out.

But caregiving will also change the way you *feel*.

In the previous two chapters, I talked about embracing the job of caregiving and looking after some caregiving essentials. In many ways, it is about filling gaps and making sure you get the things done that have to be done. But as your older parent starts approaching the end of his or her life, it's about more than just getting things done. The process of aging and decline also means it is time to make sense of life, emotionally reckon with losses, grieve through the death of friends and family members, and eventually let go of everything, including life itself. In other words, the aging process is also about the emotional work that must be done. In this chapter, I'll discuss the emotional aspect of what the decline toward the end of life may mean for you and your aging parent.

Dealing with Depression

Depression is sometimes referred to as the "common cold" of mental disorders because it is amazingly common. One in every three people will experience some type of depression in their lives. And depression is not just the blues or some emotional downturn; depression is a serious condition that means the sufferer cannot experience pleasure and often feels lifeless, dull, sad, or oppressed. Depression also affects a person's biological well-being in that a sufferer may unintentionally lose or gain weight, will be unable to sleep or will sleep all the time, will feel extremely agitated or will be fatigued, and feel painful sensations in his or her body.

Depression is a deep trough, and it's especially common in older people – at least two times as common as in the general population. If you think that suicide risk is the most prevalent in the adolescent population, think again. Elders are most at risk and far more successful at suicide than any other group.

Why are older people more at risk for depression? Most likely because of several factors common to both aging and depression. First, there is the factor of psychological loss. No matter how we slice it, growing old usually means we experience myriad losses, such as job and career, income earning power, financial power and resources, physical strength, cognitive ability, friends, and maybe a spouse. We particularly desire to control our environment and remain independent – but as we grow elderly, we are able to control our environment less and less.

Simply stated, the aging process is like an invasion force that attacks our ability to control, hold on, and remain independent.

The resulting losses add up to predictable reactions such as feelings of hopelessness, grief, mourning, and general sadness – all symptomatic of depression.

The second factor depression has in common with aging is chronic illness. Any person struggling with physical pain or ill health can tell you he or she often feels terrible emotionally. The body naturally girds itself up to bear pain and uses a tremendous amount of energy to compensate when we do not feel well. Most of us know the experience of "gutting it out" through a special project or an important family event, despite not feeling well. After making such a heroic effort, you typically feel absolutely spent. Imagine, then, how it feels for a person who can never escape such pain or illness. He or she may muster energy to compensate for a short time, but after a while, all the resources of energy get spent. The result is fatigue, pain, and sickness, with no way to escape. The pain pounds the body like a prize fighter pounds an opponent on the ropes. With each day, he or she feels worse and worse.

Aging people in decline are particularly susceptible to chronic conditions. Imagine what it's like to live year after year with heart disease, impaired lung capacity, or diabetes. Then add to these problems issues such as pain from chronic arthritis, stomach and bowel disturbances, muscle pain, and fractures. It's easy to imagine how the process of aging sets up people to live for years with chronic illnesses and pain. And as the pain persists year after year, the emotional and energy resources used to stay on an even keel eventually disappear, opening the door to deep depression.

A third contributor to depression is undoubtedly brain chemistry. Although we still know far less about the brain than what we'd like, we do know there is a marked difference in brain activity between depressed people and others who aren't depressed. The brain uses chemical messengers to communicate from one brain cell to the next, so it is reasonable to assume that differences in brain activity are, at least in part, due to this chemical activity. In the broadest sense, depression and brain activity are believed to be linked in three possible ways:

- the primary chemical (serotonin) that makes the brain cells activate gets in short supply or is not produced at all, leaving the person feeling emotionally blunted
- the brain cells activate but have trouble receiving messages from one another; even though the brain cells are active, they don't effectively communicate and thus the chemical messages aren't received, resulting in a brain dysfunction
- the brain cells activate but then quickly reabsorb the chemical messenger designed to pass along messages to the next cell

The problem, of course, is that as yet we have no way to measure the brain chemicals or directly observe the interactions of brain cells. As a result, we have to surmise the way the brain functions, especially with regard to the issue of depression.

We do know, though, that most aging people lose brain cells and produce fewer of the chemicals that make these brain cells function effectively. There is little doubt that the aging brain is more susceptible to chemical imbalance, and thus aging individuals are more prone to depression.

Finally, we know that as death approaches, a person begins to review his or her life and ponder the legacy that he or she will leave behind. In many cases, this process is positive as the person comes to terms with relational connections made, good things experienced, lessons learned, and wisdom gained. But for many, there comes the realization of opportunities lost, relationships neglected, and failure to make a difference. As a result, the person often feels as though his or her life was meaningless, and therefore change seems hopeless. In the field of aging, this conclusion is called *despair* and is almost synonymous with depression.

Treating Depression

No matter the cause or connection between depression and aging, depression can and should be treated. Sadly, aging individuals do face some discrimination. It's as though we look at an older parent and think, "Of course you feel depressed. You're old, and that's what happens when you get old." As caregivers, we must recognize that the state of depression is *not* normal (even if it is common) and that to leave the condition untreated can have serious health effects on our loved ones.

Dealing with Loss

Just because the process of aging makes some loss inevitable doesn't mean nothing can be done. All of us experience loss throughout our lives, and we've come to see that even though losses make us feel sad, they teach us valuable lessons that add to our repertoire of wisdom. We also know that even though some losses hurt deeply, we can grieve the loss and remember the goodness of what the lost relationship or object meant to us. In other words, everything about loss that hurts us causes pain because those things and relationships have added to our lives.

Such is the case when elders feel loss. The problem, of course, is that they may have no assistance in recounting the wisdom that comes with loss, grieving the sadness over the loss, and discovering the goodness of what the relationships or objects meant. We can help them by talking about these issues with our aging parents.

Here are a few of the kinds of questions you can ask to

help connect the elder with the wisdom of relationships and experiences:

- What lessons have you learned from your experiences on the job?
- What was the most valuable characteristic of that family member or friend who just passed away?
- How do you feel about life now, having learned what you now know?
- How did that particular experience make a difference in the way you lived?

As your older parent remembers, no doubt pain and tears will come. Be willing to cry along with him or her as he or she recalls these stories. The apostle Paul's advice is so wise: "Rejoice with those who rejoice; mourn with those who mourn. Live in harmony with one another" (Romans 12:15–16). And finally, be sure to affirm the value of this exercise of talking through the past.

Loss is difficult, but it doesn't take away our hope. In the larger sense, loss points toward the fact that this world and life as we know it will pass away, giving way to the new hope we have in Jesus Christ. As Paul declares, "We do not want you to be ignorant about those who fall asleep, or to grieve like the rest of men, who have no hope" (1 Thessalonians 4:13). Embracing this hope doesn't mean we deny grief; it doesn't imply that our elders will not grieve. What Paul teaches us is this: the process of experiencing grief and enduring pain eventually brings us to the promise of eternity in the presence of Jesus, where loss is a thing of the past.

Get Moving

If you've ever been really depressed, then you understand how difficult and traumatic "getting moving" can be. It is a little like having the constant physical misery of the flu, mixed with an overwhelming, hopeless expectation that each hour is going to feel just a little bit worse. Surely this is something of what Job must have felt as he dealt with depression and loss: "My eyes have grown dim with grief; my whole frame is but a shadow" (Job 17:7). Stated simply, depression feels awful and makes you feel like doing nothing.

We know, however, that there is value in stimulating the body and the brain through simple activity. For elders, it's especially important to develop some type of routine—to do simple things such as getting up and going to bed at regular times, eating regularly prepared meals, doing exercise or physical therapy, reading or being read to, doing simple projects, and taking care of basic hygiene needs. It may seem like little things, but routine tends to help depressed people get to the next mile marker.

One elderly woman once said to me, "If I stay in bed, I will feel bad. If I get up, I will still feel bad, but I will get something accomplished. I might as well get something accomplished." This attitude helped her persist through difficult times despite her emotional struggle. By following this routine, eventually her depression lifted.

Physical activity usually won't have an immediate effect on depression, but research reveals that it can shorten the duration of depression.

Medications Can Help

It always surprises me that people often refuse to medicate older people who are in chronic pain or depression. It's almost as though we believe that the aging process *should* include depression and pain.

I am well aware that medications can have serious side effects —especially in an elderly person, who has a more fragile brain and body. But the reality is that we live in a remarkable day when we have available all sorts of medications that have tremendous results.

Do these medications carry risks? Certainly they do. Even in simple cases such as taking an allergy medication to stop a runny nose and itchy eyes, there's a risk of causing drowsiness or raising blood pressure a bit. But the relief gained from the medication usually outweighs the risk. Each older parent is different, and the relief from pain and depression must always be evaluated in tandem with potential risks, but in most cases, pain and depression are such serious matters that they warrant the risk of taking medication.

Having said that though, there is no guarantee that medications for pain and depression will work the same way in every person. These aren't magic formulas. This is especially true with psychotropic medications – the kind of medications used to treat depression. No blood test can reveal whether your loved one has a chemical imbalance. A medical doctor typically will prescribe an antidepressant medication and slowly build the dose over a few days or weeks. He or she will then periodically evaluate your older parent through the first few months to determine if the medication is doing any good and will adjust dosages along the way. If the physician determines there is no improvement, then he or she will likely try a different antidepressant. With each new medication, the same procedure is followed – building dosage and blood levels of the medication, followed by evaluation, followed by adjustment. If this sounds a bit like trial and error, you're beginning to get the picture. Physicians certainly have great experience and expertise when it comes to prescribing, and they use their best judgment to prescribe what may work best. But no physician can guarantee what medication will work. He or she has to work with each older person to find an effective intervention for that individual.

Since this experience and expertise is so important, it is essential that the prescribing physician have some kind of specialization with a geriatric population. Most often, psychiatrists will be the ones to prescribe antidepressants; but increasingly, a variety of physicians have the expertise to address depression pharmacologically. Whether the prescribing physician is a psychiatrist, internist, general practitioner, or family doctor, he or she needs to have geriatric experience and know how psychotropic medications can affect the older brain.

Resolving Old Issues

It's a sad thing to come to the end of your life, only to realize you have lived for all the wrong things. If you think only non-Christians come to the end of life with deep regret, then you are profoundly wrong. Many Christians come to the end of life with deeply broken relationships with family members, enmity between themselves and friends, and a feeling of having dedicated themselves to things of no eternal value. The feeling of a life lived for the wrong reasons (or for unsuccessful causes) can rob us of hope and leave hopelessness in its wake. Surely this is something of what the prophet Jeremiah must have felt as he dealt with the pain of his own life's circumstances: "I remember my affliction and my wandering, the bitterness and the gall. I well remember them, and my soul is downcast within me" (Lamentations 3:19–20).

I once worked with a woman named Doris. By all reports, Doris was a self-absorbed woman with a reputation as a judgmental nag. Out of obligation her daughter and son took turns visiting her, but they had no real connection. I have little doubt that Doris would have slipped out of this life deeply depressed, without saying a word that made a difference to her children. I spent some time with Doris talking about her life and what it meant for her to come to the end of life. She complained, "I've done the best I could, and I feel like my children don't want to be around me." I acknowledged her pain and said, "I'm sure you've done the best you could. It is seldom the case that someone does less. The question I usually have, however, is, 'Now that you are older and wiser, are there things you wish you would have done differently?'"

Doris thought for a couple of minutes and then responded, "I've often been a hard woman. I should have been softer to my children and not so demanding." I took her hand and said, "Well, if you believe you should have been softer in the past, it would probably mean something to your children if you were softer to them now." We talked for almost an hour about specific ways she could act more kindly toward her children when they visited. I suggested she could be more appreciative of their efforts, complain and demand less, and make more physical contact with them. To be honest, I wasn't sure Doris would take and apply the suggestions — but about a week later, her daughter dropped by my office.

"My mom mentioned that you had spoken with her," she said. "I don't know what has happened to her, but whatever you've told her has seemed to make her a little bit, I don't know, I guess the word is *sweeter*. I never thought I could say that about my mother, but as I was leaving, she gave me a hug and told me she thought I was really something. She has *never* done that before."

Doris made a similar "sweeter" connection with her son. Although her depression didn't totally lift, it did recede as she made a better connection with her children and took some steps to right old wrongs. But even if her depression never totally lifted, her children were in a much better place as a result of Doris's efforts to resolve old issues.

"You can't teach an old dog new tricks," the old saying goes — which I say is simply hogwash. Older people *can* learn new behaviors and resolve old issues. Where the elder has caused emotional pain or has regrets about the way he or she has lived, it is never too late to try to address and resolve these old issues. At worst, these efforts are evidence of a wish for things to improve. At best, these efforts — no matter how infirm or old the loved one is — present an opportunity to resolve long-standing issues that, left untended, can breed depression, loneliness, and pain in the hearts of generations to come.

Dealing with Dementia

As we age, debilitating dementia certainly isn't a guaranteed malady. Although aging brings some normal decline in memory — especially short-term memory — chances are actually quite low that we will experience any profound dementia by our seventies. But as we reach our eighties, chances of severe brain dysfunction increase exponentially. In fact, prospects may be as high as 50 percent that people aged eighty-five and older will develop dementia, with by far the majority contracting Alzheimer's disease.

There is simply no way to adequately describe the pain of having a parent, who has loved you, shown interest in every part of your life, and wanted nothing more than to know your heart, look at you and have absolutely no idea who you are. Dementia is a black hole that robs your older parent not only of his or her memories but also of cognitive abilities, reasoning functions, coping skills, and eventually his or her total personality. It is what family social science expert Pauline Boss calls an "ambiguous loss."* You see the person whom you loved disappear and become a shell. Your parent is still "here," but somehow the person you knew as Mom or Dad is gone. And it doesn't happen all at once. Dementia is an insidious, mean process that does its thievery over long years — which makes it all the more painful. It is a grief process that takes a hundred miles — one inch at a time.

---

* Pauline Boss, *Ambiguous Loss* (Cambridge, Mass.: Harvard Univ. Press, 1999).

Not all dementia stems from Alzheimer's disease. Some dementia can be caused by side effects of medications. Other simple causes are poor nutrition, chronic pain, or general deterioration of health. These issues can be discovered and corrected, and your older parent may return to generally good brain function. Dementia can also be caused by some kind of brain trauma that kills brain cells, most often a stroke—an interruption of blood flow to a certain part of the brain, resulting in the "starving" off of oxygen to neurons. Strokes can cause massive brain dysfunction in motor and intellectual skills and can produce profound dementia. It is not unusual for older parents to experience minor strokes that can cause much smaller motor and intellectual impairments, but their accumulated effect can result in significant dementia.

But the cognitive threat to older people is Alzheimer's disease—a progressive disease that renders brain neurons useless, as plaque eventually kills the brain cell. As more and more brain cells get eliminated, cognitive processing ability, judgment, perception, and ability to care for oneself diminishes. Eventually, when enough brain cells die that the brain can no longer manage the body's most basic functions, death results. It is a particularly mean disease that strips away every part of the older person's self before it claims his or her life.

We don't know exactly what causes Alzheimer's, although there are a few genetic markers that may indicate its cause. Diagnosing Alzheimer's remains difficult, though some strides are being made. Prohibitive costs still make a definitive diagnosis unlikely. Most people discover their aging parent has Alzheimer's simply by noticing telltale symptoms, doing mental exams, ruling out other possible causes of impaired thinking, and watching for the progression of impairment. The following table shows some of the warning signs of Alzheimer's:

Memory loss affecting job skills	Forgets job tasks or gets confused on the job
Difficulty performing familiar tasks	Forgets a task in the middle of its execution, as in preparing a meal, or is confused or distracted by tasks formerly accomplished with little problem
Language problems	Language sometimes doesn't make sense, or forgets words or has words "on the tip of the tongue"
Disorientation with time and place	Becomes lost easily, even around common and familiar locations like work or home, or may get confused as to current location
Poor or decreased judgment	Makes poor or unsuitable choices, such as wearing inappropriate clothing (e.g., using a bathrobe as a coat)
Problems with abstract thinking	Forgets or has trouble with simple calculations that formerly posed no problem
Problems misplacing things	Loses things often but also places objects in inappropriate places (e.g., placing purse in the refrigerator) and has no idea how they got there
Mood and behavior changes	Has frequent mood swings for no apparent reason or develops new and inappropriate behavior
Changes in personality	Experiences dramatic changes in personality, such as becoming anxious and paranoid, when formerly responded in a calm and easygoing manner
Loss of initiative	Has diminished interests in activities or withdraws and becomes uninvolved in things that formerly brought great enjoyment

If your older parent displays some of these symptoms, you should seek the help of a doctor, who will likely seek to rule out other causes such as medications and diet and then order a mental status exam and perhaps an MRI scan of the brain to detect any evidence of a stroke. In rare cases, a neurologist may order a spinal tap to rule out an infection. The mental status exam will measure how your parent performs on simple memory tasks such as counting backwards or remembering words after a certain amount of time has elapsed, performing simple math calculations, reciting current dates or events, and recognizing or drawing familiar objects. In the event of impaired performance, another mental status exam will likely be ordered after a few months have elapsed. If evidence exists of further impairment in thinking, memory, and reasoning, the likely diagnosis will be Alzheimer's disease.

Some drugs have shown an ability to slow the progression of the plaque that kills brain cells, and the doctor who makes the diagnosis may prescribe these medications, but be aware that they don't cure the disease. No current treatment is yielding a cure or even a reversal of symptoms.

The disease will progress in stages. Although some professionals delineate many stages of progression for Alzheimer's, I find it helpful to think of three basic stages:

- **First Phase**. Here your older parent has progressive memory loss and has a hard time finding the right words. You may also see some substantial changes in his or her mood, and he or she may lose interest in normal activities or hobbies.

- **Middle Phase**. As your older parent progresses in the disease, he or she will likely have difficulty making decisions about clothing or food. He or she will have more mood swings and problem behaviors resulting from anger, agitation, or anxiety. Wandering occurs more often. Speech and language problems will likely increase, as well as difficulty with coordination in walking, dressing, and eating. Short-term memory will normally have ceased to function, and he or she will forget friends' names and formerly familiar places such as church.

- **End Phase**. In this phase, cognitive processes have deteriorated to the point where function is undependable. Mood swings and language will not make sense, nor will they be connected to anything in particular. Coordination deteriorates, and your older parent will eventually lose the ability to perform any motion, such as walking or eating. Long-term memory eventually is erased to the point where your older parent will no longer recognize you or any other person. In this stage, the older person is vulnerable to other life-threatening diseases or infections, but barring those, the elder will eventually die as Alzheimer's eliminates the brain's ability to control basic body functions such as respiration and heartbeat.

Physical Care and Mood Swings

With any form of profound dementia, the deeper you drill routine into rote memory, the longer the memory function may remain. All of us do many things, such as tying a shoelace, typing on a keyboard, or playing a musical instrument, without ever thinking about the specific functions. These functions are examples of deep memory skills, which often are the last to disappear with Alzheimer's disease.

For this reason, it is most beneficial to help move your loved one into some fairly strict regimens and routines. In dressing, for instance, focus on a limited number of similar clothing items because many choices tend to produce confusion. Hygiene needs should be narrowed to basics such as brushing teeth and brushing hair. Utensils for meals should be culled down to one or maybe two utensils, with one plate at a time of very simple food. Medications should be simplified – one pill at a time, with the elder learning how to take the medication immediately. Exercise and flexibility stretching should be simple but regular. All of these routines build skill memory, which provides much more resilience than reasoning power or short-term memory does.

It's difficult to fathom the profound change that happens in someone suffering from a stroke or Alzheimer's disease. The sweet, caring mother who always was so sensitive to your needs or the giving and sacrificing father who always sought first what was best for you now becomes angry, agitated, anxious, selfish, reclusive, or aggressive.

Some make the tragic mistake of believing that these behaviors and motivations were somehow latent in the personalities of their loved ones, and now the dementia is simply revealing the "true self" of the parent. Nothing could be further from the truth. Stroke and Alzheimer's disease are brain altering and are best thought of as brain injuries. In case of injury, the brain is forced to reorganize and reroute itself – a very difficult process for even a young person, but with the limitations of aging neurons, the fragility of an elder's brain, and no new brain cells being generated, it is almost impossible for an elderly brain to reorganize itself effectively. Therefore, the dysfunctional expressions and actions of your aging parent – often unpredictable and always totally incompatible with the person he or she was in earlier days – are, plainly and simply, symptomatic of the disease.

Two effective measures can be taken in cases of unreasonable and unrecognizable behaviors and mood swings. The first is the use of the class of psychotropic drugs prescribed to manage anxiety and calm aggressive moods. Many of these drugs were tested originally on younger populations, so it is possible that some of these medications will simply complicate mood and personality changes and possibly even heighten brain damage. But most psychotropic medications have been available for years and have been used successfully with older people. While it is wise to proceed with caution and understand the risks when your older parent begins to take medications to manage mood, most reactions are predictable, and you and your loved one may well see benefits from a more stable mood and personality.

The second measure is to undertake a modification of the environment. For instance, in the middle phases of her Alzheimer's disease, my mother-in-law became very agitated and anxious about issues of "time." She would constantly focus on the time on her watch and the clock in her room. For some reason, she would pace, get people's attention, and fret about the time, even though nothing in particular needed to be done. The solution? Remove her watch and clock—and within weeks, her anxiety decreased markedly.

If your loved one with Alzheimer's does something destructive in a particular room, such as turning on the water or taking apart the toilet, then take steps to limit access to that room. If medication times or mealtimes become tense or aggressive, then experiment with doing something different in a different place to see if the situation calms down. In other words, make any changes necessary in order to reduce agitation and aggression until the issue passes.

Eventually, an older person with Alzheimer's disease will need twenty-four-hour care. Many caregivers choose to keep the Alzheimer's elder in their own home and provide the necessary level of care. While this may suit some, the substantial emotional and physical toll on you and the home has to be recognized. You need not feel guilty if you decide to opt for a care facility when your loved one reaches this stage of intense caregiving.

The Gradient of Care and Control

Since older people – in reality, all individuals – are happiest when they maintain as much independence as possible, it makes sense to try to maintain that sense of control for your aging parent who suffers from dementia. Except with early onset of Alzheimer's, which usually has a very quick course of deterioration, your aging parent will most likely lose control of his or her abilities slowly, over a period of months and years.

Keep in mind two core issues as the dementia progresses: (1) the gradual nature of the decline of your loved one and (2) the gradient of how much control you will need to exercise in the caregiving process. For a substantial amount of time at the beginning stages of her disease, for instance, my mother-in-law was able to order her prescriptions from the drugstore and accurately take those medications on her own. I would keep careful counts of her medication each week to verify that she was taking it properly. She was able to get the right medication 90 to 95 percent of the time.

As her decline accelerated, however, she could no longer confidently manage the call-in prescriptions. I took over ordering her medicines and placing them in a daily medication box. Although she had deteriorated significantly, she was still independent enough to locate the medication box, keep track of the day of the week, and take her medication on her own. But as she became confused with time and space, I had to make arrangements for her to be given her medication and supervised to make sure she actually took what she was given. There is a point, in other words, when the gradual nature of the decline of your elderly parent meets with the gradient of increase of need for care – a point when you will become more in control of your parent than he or she is of himself or herself.

In my opinion, it is best to help your loved one maintain

control of his or her care for as long as possible. It contributes to the elder's adjustment and a sense of satisfaction that comes only from independence. Soon enough you will become responsible for your parent with dementia, and so any independence that can be maintained on the front end is less time when the elder will totally depend on you.

Emotional Connection and Grief

When a person in full control of his or her cognition approaches death, he or she often will be very intentional about saying or doing things that connect to family members. Sometimes it is the passing along of wisdom in "last words," or the parent's sharing of words that show how much confidence he or she has in the adult child.

But one of the insidious things about dementia in general and Alzheimer's disease in particular is the disappearance of this ability to connect and say meaningful things. To make matters more confusing, it disappears so gradually that people often wait too long to make the connections they deeply desire.

A rather peculiar bond exists between a caregiver and an elder with Alzheimer's. At one moment, the caregiver begs and prays for relief from the caregiving job; in the next moment, feelings of displacement and underappreciation surface when the intense caregiving is no longer needed. *Realize that the day will come when your parent with Alzheimer's will no longer recognize you.* It will be a hard and emotional day, but it will be easier if you have made the connections in advance of that day. Speak words of affirmation and appreciation to your parent when he or she is still cognitively able to understand and respond. Hold on tightly while your parent has the ability to recognize you and cling to you. One piece at a time, the disease will suck him or her away from you. If you are waiting for the "right time" to make that connection or say those words, then it's quite likely you are waiting too long.

Be willing to make emotional connections even when the dementia is advanced. I once took Genevieve on a walk at a time when she had very little language skill left. We sat on a bench in the park and watched the ducks in the pond sail by. I reached over and took her hand. Although she didn't say a word, she took my hand and studied it as though she was reviewing for a history exam. She seemed to be saying, "I don't know *how* this is important, but I know that it is indeed important." It was a sweet time of connecting with Genevieve—the experience of an intimacy beyond verbal communication.

Always be willing to sit, hold, talk to, and connect, even when it appears that your elder is unable to do so. At some point, you will likely make a connection that you thought had become impossible.

Dealing with Death

Death is one of the unavoidable realities about aging. Even though we may not wish to talk about death—and we live in a society that abhors the very thought of dying—the topic demands careful thought and substantial planning. Any caregiver who chooses to disregard death until it actually happens is simply refusing to acknowledge the proverbial elephant sitting in the living room.

I point out this avoidance, but I do not judge it. Our society carefully trains us to give death no consideration. Families in past centuries handled death much more openly. Burial preparation took place in the home. Accidents, injuries, and simple illnesses claimed a much greater percentage of lives than they do today. But as medical science began to cure life-threatening illnesses and treatment at hospitals became more common, our culture began to take the deathbed out of the home. Burial prep-aration went over to professionals, and ever since, our society has become less and less comfortable with the subject.

But make no mistake – both your aging parent and you will eventually die: "By the sweat of your brow you will eat your food until you return to the ground, since from it you were taken; for dust you are and to dust you will return" (Genesis 3:19). As Christians, we often think we can escape death, and in part it's true. But while we escape spiritual death and ultimate separation from God, *all* humans will experience the physical pain of having our bodies die and the temporary ripping apart of soul from body.

Be Thoughtful about Death

When dealing with the impending death of aging parents, care-givers must face the important issue of how to manage the care up until the time of death. While I don't advocate *any* type of euthanasia, I recognize that we cannot and should not try to permanently stave off death, especially when it has become clear that our loved one has come to the end of his or her life story. I believe it is a sin to murder. No mere human can make the decision to end another's life; that right belongs only to God. I am equally convinced, however, that it is a sin to try to keep someone alive past his or her time to die. David tells us that God determines each person's life span: "All the days ordained for [us] were written in [God's] book before one of them came to be" (Psalm 139:16).

Medical science has advanced to the point where we are much more likely than previous generations to try to keep people alive past their time to die. I sometimes think that because *we* don't want to face death and judgment, we want to avoid this reality for our elders. As a result, we take extreme measures to keep them "living" – performing unnecessary surgeries with no hope of positive recovery, resuscitating elders who will suffer with profound brain or organ damage, or engaging in expensive treatments to preserve life for only a few more days or weeks.

I believe we must come to grips with the idea of when "enough is enough." If we're unclear about the treatments we and our loved ones think are prudent, then medical professionals will often continue to treat patients. Although I know many physicians who subtly try to help the caregiver back away from medical procedures that offer little or no hope, I believe it is the caregiver's responsibility to come to most of these conclusions by asking thoughtful and clear questions.

In our case, Sharon and I could have kept her mother alive for many weeks after Alzheimer's had robbed her of the ability to swallow by consenting to have a feeding tube inserted. She might have held on for months, but certainly she would have shown no improvement. It wasn't that we were anxious to see Genevieve die; we were simply acknowledging that her condition had deteriorated to the point where the disease would take its natural course and bring her life to an end. Was it a hard decision? Did some people not understand it? Yes to both questions, but we knew the time had come for Genevieve to pass, and so we let the natural course of the disease take her.

Even if you decide to take more drastic measures with your loved one than we did, you will have to reasonably formulate your position and not be easily persuaded to continue medical treatment just because *you* want to avoid thinking about death.

Be Prepared for Death

Our cultural denial of death has made us hesitant or uncomfortable about talking with our elders about death. It would be nice if our parents brought up the subject – but it rarely happens. This job usually falls to the caregiver. I always encourage the caregiver to bring to the fore what I call the "logistics" of death – funeral details, finances, and beliefs about death.

Funeral details are just the nitty-gritty of the preparations for a funeral and the elder's wishes for that funeral. Some elders make very specific prepaid arrangements with funeral directors to ensure that this burden doesn't land on the caregiver or family; others make no plans at all.

In my opinion, preplanning is always a better option and usually results in better decisions. Reputable funeral homes (check with your Better Business Bureau – seriously!) will have preplanning arrangements that allow you and your elder to make decisions that fit your budget and wishes – but first you must get your loved one to talk about what he or she wants. Do not accept the statements "you just decide" or "whatever you think is best." Ask thoughtful questions such as, "In funerals you've attended, what did you like and dislike? What kind of music would you like? What kind of Scripture verses and sermons do you like to hear at funerals? What comforted you?" Remember that you, the caregiver, will be present at the funeral, so you should feel free to give your opinions. Talking about these issues is usually the easiest way to begin discussing death, and doing so can open the door to important discussions about finances and beliefs.

Finances are always a touchy subject, but these discussions become especially difficult around the time of death because (1) there is the inevitable fact that bills must be paid, and (2) the remaining assets and "stuff" must be divided. As caregiver, you need to make sure your elder has a current will. Wills often sit untouched for decades, despite substantial changes that take place in the finances of the family or in the physical condition of your loved one. It is very important that the will state who the *executor* of the estate will be and that the executor is well equipped to carry out the job. An executor is a person appointed to carry out the wishes of the deceased and to handle all the affairs of the estate. The executor has to probate the will after the person's death to attest that all debts have been paid, affairs have been settled, and the wishes of the deceased have been fulfilled. It is often a time-consuming job, and sometimes caregivers who have given of themselves for years aren't willing to go through the work of being an executor. However, the caregiver is typically the best informed as to the financial condition of the loved one and his or her wishes.

The will usually addresses property and large assets, as well as specifics regarding who disposes of personal effects. Do not underestimate the power of this personal "stuff" and the potential for harm and broken relationships! I have seen families go to war over something as simple as Mom's or Dad's eyeglasses. It is best if you help your elderly parent go through personal items and specify who in the family should receive particular objects and mementoes. These conclusions can be attached to the will or simply placed as a written instruction from the older parent to the executor of the will. If the elder is not able (or simply refuses) to make this determination, I've seen executors gather all direct relatives after the loved one passes and implement a sequential selection process, from oldest to youngest, on individual personal items. When everyone has selected one item, the process begins again until all the items formerly belonging to the elder are taken. While such a process works, I believe it robs the elder and caregiver of some of the joy and positive experience of connecting items with family members and making the process more meaningful. Still, if the elder does not wish to specify who gets what, this arrangement can help to head off protracted family conflicts.

The final issue in preparing the aging parent for death is to talk specifically about *beliefs*. Some frightened elders don't know what to expect from the process of physical decline; others have deep spiritual questions about how death occurs and what happens to the soul after death. Although no mere human being can give absolute answers to many of these questions, pastors, leaders, doctors, nurses, and friends can often give great comfort through well-considered answers. Such a discussion often supplies the opportunity for the loved one to hear the gospel. Even older adults who previously rejected the gospel of Christ can become open to grace once they have tasted advanced age and approaching death. It is never too late to accept God's grace during one's lifetime on earth, and we should always be willing to engage in conversations about impending death to ensure clarity about that grace or to give one more opportunity for the elder to gain access to that grace.

At the Time of Death

Most people wish to die suddenly in their sleep just after they've completed the "useful" parts of their lives. I hope these chapters have convinced you that medical advances have made it unlikely that you will die quickly after you reach a certain age. We typically will decline slowly into death, much as an airplane makes a slow descent to the runway.

In fact, it's quite likely that your aging parent will be under some form of medical care for quite some time as he or she winds down toward death. At some point, if the decline continues, a doctor will likely inform you that there is nothing more to be done and a referral will be made to a hospice. Hospice organizations are designed to help dying people proceed through the process with dignity, connection, and intimacy. Whether for-profit or nonprofit, hospices are committed to the idea of serving terminal patients with compassionate care. Hospice professionals can help you care for your aging parent when he or she is close to death, take steps to make him or her as comfortable and pain free as possible, and provide you with hands-on information about the process of death. Most hospices also provide you with emotional support and caring through the entire process. If your parent has Medicare, most services provided by a hospice will be paid for by that insurance. I have found hospice organizations and workers to be first-rate and extremely caring. You may choose to go through the dying process without a hospice, but at least be aware of the support and care available should you care to access it at some time.

When the moment of death comes for a loved one, I often find it helpful for caregivers to give "presence" and "permission." I believe an elder can often sense when a caregiver is not ready to let him or her go. There are times when caregivers go home to eat dinner or get some rest, only to receive word that the parent has died. I often wonder if the parent was simply waiting for the opportunity to be alone in order to make it a bit easier on the caregiver. I've seen this phenomenon take place both when the older parent is conscious and when he or she is unconscious.

I believe it helps to give the older parent permission to die. When we knew that Genevieve was very close to death, Sharon, her brother John, and I were present for her last few hours. As was her habit in her mother's last few months, Sharon crawled into bed with her mother, stroked her hair, and held her with a big hug across her middle. "I love you, Mom," she said as she pulled her mother close. John, holding his mother's hand on her other side, said, "It's OK to let go, Mom. We will be OK." Sitting beside her pillow, I gently stroked her cheek and said, "It has been a tough road, but you've made it. We will see you in heaven." Sharon added, "You will be free, with your mind healed and you'll be dancing in heaven." John reaffirmed, "Yes."

Genevieve breathed two full breaths and then one short half breath, as if to hold the presence of love in the room. Then she was gone, slipping out of our hands into the presence of the living God as easily as a raindrop gliding off a flower petal. I have seen this phenomenon many times with other caregivers and elders. It is a powerful moment of passing. It is also a privilege to hold on to our elders as they grab hold of God.

PART 2

THE
CHALLENGE
OF

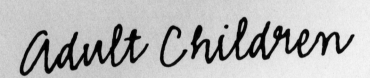

4

WHAT HAPPENED TO MY EMPTY NEST?

I hope you are seeing that the times are indeed a-changin'. The challenges presented by caregiving for aging parents aren't simply some additional responsibilities that will bring difficult times for the "sandwich generation." In fact, these challenges represent a major shift in the way family will be "done" for the rest of this century and a significant modification in the way in which people in their retirement years will live.

At the same time that this sociological change is taking place at the tail end of life, another one is occurring at the front end of adulthood. Many adult children who thirty years ago would have been moving out and starting careers, marriages, and families are now caught in a holding pattern.

And many will return home to live with you.

While medical science has been the primary change agent responsible for bringing about longer and healthier life spans, resulting in tremendous economic implications for how we and our aging parents live, in the case of adult children returning home to live for a significant period, the primary cause has been economic. We didn't ask for these medical and economic changes, and very little in the experience of previous generations has prepared us for the big work ahead. Still, the changes aren't the result of anyone's failure, whether ours or any other group's; they simply reflect a cycle of history ordained by God to teach and train, discipline and correct.

It does fall to us, however, to make the necessary adjustments, learn from the challenges, and work out the family processes to be applied over the next several decades. As the boomer generation, we are uniquely qualified to deal with change because our generation has ushered in more than our fair share of modifications to family life, at both a personal and sociological level.

Moving Away from the "Normal" Family Life Cycle

We're accustomed to thinking that after marriage and raising young children, we will nurture our children from adolescence into adulthood and launch them into careers and families of their own. After this launching period, we will experience a time of "empty nest" when we refocus our concerns and work at greater intimacy with our spouses, deal with the decline and relatively quick death of our parents, finish our working careers, and slowly adjust to the new challenges of being in-laws and grandparents. That was "normal" – and most of us expected it. But there is a "new normal" today with new realities to face. In Part 1, we looked at the first new reality, namely, caring for our aging parents. Here in Part 2, we'll discuss the reality of raising adult children who have moved back home.

Many of our adult children are no longer able to make it on their own after graduation from high school and college. In many ways, they are pioneers with us as they explore new ways of establishing themselves and learn what it means to build committed relationships in a world that changed radically even while they were growing up.

What does it take to "get out on your own"? We typically point to three hallmarks. The first is *getting a job* that will meet the basic needs of housing, transportation, and food – not an easy task, of course, as actual wages, when adjusted for inflation, have decreased significantly while the cost of living has skyrocketed. Combine this with the fact that inexpensive housing options are much harder to come by these days, and you begin to understand why young adults find it difficult to get over this first hurdle.

The second hallmark is actually *moving out of the parents' home.* Although much of this has to do with taking economic responsibility for yourself, it also means establishing yourself emotionally as an adult. No longer do you need your parents to approve of your decisions and choices, because if you are truly on your own, then you bear the responsibility and benefit of your own choices. You emotionally claim that you are independent, free, and fully adult, no longer depending on or feeling inhibited by undue parental influence. Of course, without a way to reliably support yourself and having little choice to live anywhere but with your parents, claiming such adulthood is difficult.

"Am I still a child if I'm twenty-two years old and still live at home? Am I an adult, even though my parents have to foot the bills?" Such questions not only undermine the adult child's ability to move into adulthood but also hinder the parents as they struggle with the same questions.

The third hallmark is *moving the main source of relationships and intimacy to peers and potential mate partners.* If I'm a young adult who lives on my own, I have the opportunity to start trying out my personality and style largely unfettered by what my parents think about my behavior. My peers and potential life partners are the ones who start giving me feedback on what works or doesn't work in my personality and on where I need to grow. So when I make choices to change, I do so not because it pleases or displeases my parents but to satisfy myself.

This element is an important step toward becoming responsible for who I am as an adult and who I will eventually become as my own person. I become responsible for how my own personhood is shaped and how my personality affects my relationships. If I cannot or will not move out of my parents' home, then I have a tendency to keep the responsibility for change outside of myself — with my parents — and have difficulty accepting what is called the "internal locus of control." In other words, I'm refusing to accept that I am the motivator and implementer of my change, and I'm responsible for the effect on my relationships with my peers and mates.

Economic pressures and relational failures have essentially delayed the onset of adulthood. Young adults today are just as likely as not to move back home for a significant period of time, because they see no way to make it on their own, have tried and failed to make it on their own, or have experienced a significant relational setback, with all the financial issues that the failure brings. As a result, not only will we boomers be caring for our parents as they decline and die; we'll also have to give care in order to "finish" raising our young adult children until they launch out of our homes for good.

Not All Returning Young Adults Are the Same

No doubt many things in our world are tougher than they used to be — jobs, the state of the economy, and decent housing. Some may even argue that relationships are harder. But the truth is, not all adult kids return home for the same reasons. Although *our* goals in helping our adult kids move into full-fledged adult-hood may differ little from child to child, we should recognize that our kids will have different motivations for moving home.

Dealing with the Discouraged

Caesar was a good kid in his growing-up years, and he really did have big plans. He worked hard in high school and got respectable grades. He worked his way through community college and then a four-year university program, eventually earning a business degree. From his perspective, he was ready to set his sights on success and his own place in life.

But while he was a hard worker, he was far from the top student in his class and didn't get flashy internships. When recruiters visited his campus to interview prospective employees, he had trouble getting a second look. He worked hard at interviewing and tried to be flexible—looking at banking, finance, brokerage houses, insurance, and sales. But after four months of looking for a job, he still had landed nothing.

Caesar's parents were absolutely committed to getting him "out there" to achieve some type of success. While they supported him by letting him live at home, they insisted that he contribute toward paying his way.

"They asked me to pay a little rent," Caesar said. "It was OK at first because I thought it was a reasonable request and I should be able to make it fine. After all, throughout college I had a job to pay the bill for my car insurance and have some spending money."

But soon the rent turned into a resentful burden for Caesar. "When I was in college," he said, "I really didn't mind working at minimum wage to meet my overall goal. But now that I am a graduate and realized that I have to go back to my job at the restaurant, it's really discouraging. I keep wondering if I'll always be stuck in this place. Paying rent to my parents just seemed to back me into a corner of having to work at a job where I feel trapped. I have to work to pay my bills, but I really need to be out looking for a job that allows me to use my degree."

It didn't take long for Caesar to become discouraged way down to the bedrock of his soul. He began to feel as though he would never escape from his restaurant job. As a result, he became unmotivated and depressed. Because his parents saw his discouragement, they urged him to "get out more." So, to try to make himself feel better, Caesar spent more and more time hanging out with friends and going to some of his old haunts. Soon the unmotivated drag of going nowhere led him into a familiar pattern of working at his job, going out at night, sleeping late, and doing the whole thing over again the next day.

"I hate my life," he said. "Everything about what I do reminds me of being a kid in high school, and I really don't see how I'm going to break out to something different."

Back in the 1960s, when the United States had 4 percent unemployment, it was fairly easy to get a job that would pay the bills and get you to adulthood. But with unemployment chronically higher and so many college graduates on the market, getting an "adult" job is much harder than it used to be. It is easy to get discouraged, and motivation can fade after a matter of weeks and months in the face of the year or two it may take to secure significant employment.

Recognize, too, that corporate employers sometimes focus only on the bottom line and not on employees. Many will hire recent graduates, only to retain the ones who show the most potential by turning out quick results. For many others, however, the first job they get will result in termination within the first year—which is discouraging enough but also makes it doubly tough to find another position. As a result, discouraged young adults often become unmotivated and depressed. This "stuck" feeling can lead to displays of resentment, blaming, angry outbursts, and addictive behavior. While it is not Caesar's fault that he is unsuccessful, it is clear that he must keep working at getting himself motivated and out of his parents' house.

Were Caesar's parent's wrong for making him pay rent? Well, they certainly had the correct intention. They didn't realize, though, that the simple request to pay a little rent would add to Caesar's discouragement and depression. His old job did not make him responsible; in fact, he was already responsible. More than anything else, Caesar needed encouragement, patience, and the empathetic recognition that the world had become a different place. He isn't stuck at home because he is unwilling to work; he is stuck because he doesn't know how to get himself out of his current situation and into a successful and secure position. In other words, he is applying the wrong solutions to his problem and as a result may remain unsuccessful for a long time.

When I look at the current crop of adult kids living at home, I see a group of young adults who seem very discouraged – and this discouragement is their primary problem.

Dealing with the Ill-Equipped

Julie is a bright and vivacious twenty-three-year-old who seemingly has nothing stopping her from pursuing whatever she wants. In high school, she rose to the top of her class and was accepted to a prestigious program in a state school. She was a top-notch music student, a very good athlete, and very popular with classmates and teachers.

But when Julie went away to college, she didn't quite fit in. She got only mediocre grades and continually complained to her parents about feeling unhappy and unfulfilled. She made few friends and often came home on the weekends. Her parents made positive suggestions, often went to see her, and tried to figure out just what was hindering her from finding direction. They asked her to get a physical exam, sent her to counseling, and even went with her to some family counseling sessions.

Although Julie came close to failing a couple of classes, she always scraped by. She simply didn't excel in *any* of her classes. Her interest in school waned as she tried out several majors, seeking to discover her calling in life. After four majors but still several credit hours short of a degree, she became totally discouraged, lost interest in college, and returned home.

"She is so bright, and she seems to be right on the edge of being able to get it together," her mother said. "But instead she has trouble being motivated and is confused about what career would be the best for her. We want to encourage her, but we're at a loss in trying to help her get started."

Julie expressed a similar sentiment: "I know there are so many things I could do, but I have trouble just settling in and finding something I really have a passion for. Each time I start something, it just seems like I'm settling for less than the best. I don't want to start something that isn't suited for me."

Boomers love their children; this is a positive, not a negative. Our parents also loved us and wanted us to have more than they did, but when we boomers were small, our choices were undeniably more limited. Most of us had few choices when it came to the school we attended, the athletic choices we had, our cultural opportunities, and travel options. We went to our neighborhood school, participated in seasonal sports, and maybe took part in a very select few opportunities offered in our communities.

In the world in which we raised our children, however, choices have mushroomed almost to the point of becoming unlimited. In education, for instance, our children not only had choices as to what kind of school—public, private, home school, Christian, boarding school—but also had multiple program choices within those schools, such as international baccalaureate, advanced placement, gifted and talented, and honors. Many more athletic choices are available now as well, and the demand has grown for advanced lessons and skill-building opportunities in these sports throughout the year. It is not unusual in the area of the country where I live, for example, to start girls in volleyball at a very young age, have them participate on traveling club teams year-round, and expose them to special camps and lessons to prepare them to compete at the high school level. The same choices are available with lessons for any kind of musical instrument, voice lessons, theater training, and art classes, just to name a few.

Boomers wanted their children to accomplish more and have more opportunities than they had, just as their own parents wanted for them. But the sheer volume of choices often felt overwhelming to those children and made it difficult for them to find themselves. Believing that our children shouldn't miss any opportunity or privilege, we boomers usually overinvolved them with activities, trying to make sure they were "equipped." In turn, when our children got overwhelmed with the burden of schoolwork, athletics, and activities, we usually stepped in and helped them out of the mess. Too often when things got difficult, we boomers filled the gaps and made all the connections work; after all, hadn't we encouraged our children to participate in the activities in the first place?

Although our hearts were in the right place as we raised our children, this feverish work to provide multiple opportunities has had an undesirable effect on many boomer children. Many of these kids were raised to believe that they could do anything they wanted and that participating at a high level was only a matter of getting the right lessons and training. Many, like Julie, came to believe that success in life would follow inevitably out of natural talent. If things became too stressful, parents would always be there to pick up the slack and give support. In an effort to give their children every opportunity, boomers have often unknowingly inundated their kids with "things" and opportunities that have led many away from finding their natural passions and talents. As a result, they have unrealistic and slanted ideas about what it takes to succeed and have trouble working through tough times when interest wanes. Worse yet, these adult kids have often not experienced enough anxiety that they themselves must respond to and solve. As a result, many have inadequate coping and problem-solving skills and tend to get perplexed and stuck when problems arise.

Julie's parents, like so many boomers, were just trying to be loving, supportive, and giving. But in the quest to give continually and offer the best, they became overinvolved in Julie's success. Instead of Julie naturally growing into her interests and passions, her parents tried to hand her those passions and interests. When she succeeded, the success itself became the motivating factor to stay involved with those activities instead of a real love for the activity and a genuine desire to continue. Like many parents of the boomer generation, Julie's mom and dad became what we call "helicopter parents" — hovering over their child to make sure everything goes well. When trouble or confusion occurs, hovering parents tend to step in quickly with suggestions and problem solving to try to find a resolution. They do none of this with malicious intentions.

Julie's parents acted in her best interest, but now Julie is suffering from being *ill-equipped* to face and deal with life's real issues. She is bright and talented, but she cannot compete and have the kind of success she experienced in high school because out in the world there are *so many* bright and talented young people. Instead of knowing what she wants, Julie moves from one subject, major, or career idea to the next, with the outlook that somehow success will "just happen" for her as it did when she was younger. Julie also lacks the problem-solving skills necessary to deal with the reality that she is an adult and will have to make adult choices. Like many adult children of boomers, Julie is under the impression that it will be fine for her to take as much time as she needs to "find" herself, because she believes her parents will be there — as they've always been there — to support her and encourage her through this time of uncertainty. This impression is well-founded, as Julie's parents seem unwilling or unable to see how they may be contributing to Julie's difficulties by trying to solve her problems for her.

If Julie is going to succeed in getting out of her parents' house and start living as an adult, she has to develop a new set of skills. It isn't so much that Julie is spoiled, but rather that she hasn't received the training necessary to make it in a world filled with choices. She will need training to help her find her own passions and to recognize and solve her own problems. Julie's parents also will have to learn to let their daughter discover her own successes and failures, as well as how to resist the temptation to step in at the first sign of trouble.

Dealing with the Lazy or Free-Spirited

Brandon is fun-loving, engaging, and the "life of the party." He's a great kid. In high school, he was always very involved with his peer group and enjoyed connecting with people. His parents divorced when he was young, but he showed little sign that it bothered him. He had a good relationship with his mother and a very close relationship with his father. In his growing-up years he had a few scrapes with drug experimentation and alcohol, but it was never anything too serious. He went to college and did OK for a couple of years but eventually got bored with the college life.

"I really didn't see where it was leading me," he said. "I

know I'll get a degree someday, but without really knowing what I wanted to do, I finally decided there wasn't any point in continuing."

He moved back home with his father and went to work in construction. All this made perfect sense to Brandon's dad: "When he told me he was unsure about what he wanted to do and that he wanted to put in a few years of work, it made great sense. I was in my late twenties before I really discovered what I wanted to do for a career."

But Brandon's father has become increasingly frustrated with his son living at home, as one year stretched into three. "His full-time job seems to be to play," he said. "He goes out with friends, goes on weekend trips skiing and such, and then he'll go on these exotic trips to Mexico or Asia for fun. He is more than happy to use my place as his base and use all of his money to pursue this carefree lifestyle."

It's not that Brandon is such a problem, but the fact is, he is making no movement to move forward with life and adulthood. He would do chores when his father asked him to, was reasonable in doing his fair share of the housework, and was careful not to ask his father to finance his fun. He also got heavily involved with his church, working as a youth middle school leader and going on several mission trips sponsored by the church. But he definitely wasn't progressing toward the goals that boomers normally associate with adulthood.

"There will come a time when I will have to work for the rest of my life," Brandon stated. "I just want to have some time to experience some of the fun things in life before I settle into a job and eventually start a family."

Brandon isn't an unusual example of his generation. Many young adults have gotten the message that life is harder as an adult and that it takes a lot of time and effort to put together a career, an independent living space, and a new circle of peer relationships. Recognizing that all this will take years, many of Brandon's generation – called *twixters* – simply delay thinking about these responsibilities and adulthood.* Instead, they prefer to see their youth as a time to try new things and have a variety of experiences before they settle into the mundane life of family and adulthood.

So what about a job, a place to live, and a circle of friends? Twixters see all these needs as already being met in the homes of their parents. Parents have a comfortable home, which these adult kids wouldn't be able to afford for at least a decade. If they stay in their parents' homes, however, they can go back to many of their adolescent relationships. And most of all, if they stay with their parents, they have the precious gift of time to do as they please without much pressure from the outside world.

If you're concluding that many in the twixter generation are taking advantage of the boomer generation, you would be correct. We may call them lazy or free-spirited, but the truth is that they simply have a way of thinking different from the one we had when we were growing into adulthood. Most boomers desired to leave home because it meant we were establishing ourselves as adults. Adulthood was desirable because of all the freedom and advantages it offered. Most twixters, on the other hand, see adulthood largely as a *challenge* to their freedom because of its increased responsibilities. In many ways, adolescence for the twixter was the epitome of the "good life" – and why would anyone want the good life to end? This mind-set explains why many twixters simply go home to relax, enjoy, and be carefree.

Brandon certainly isn't a bad kid, and much of what he does in terms of working a job and being involved in church work

---

* Lev Grossman's article "Grow Up? Not So Fast: Meet the Twixters" in the January 24, 2005, issue of *Time* magazine reflects on the generation "betwixt" adolescence and adulthood, thus the term *twixters*.

seems right on the money. It is part of the reason his father has trouble calling him irresponsible. After all, Brandon goes to work most every day, has a heart for middle school kids, and serves God—he really is doing many good things. And besides, is there anything wrong with Brandon wanting to "experience" some of life before he settles down? As a result, Brandon's father finds himself where many boomers are—facilitating their adult children's lifestyles. These lifestyles are, in many ways, appealing—they're ones we all long for. As Brandon's dad says, "Sometimes I just wish I could switch places with Brandon. His life really does look like the good life."

The problem, of course, is that the lifestyle Brandon maintains comes at his father's expense. Delaying responsibility for no good reason is like saying, "It's OK to stagnate." The Bible has a different opinion. It teaches that it is best to press on toward growth and maturity: "One thing I do: Forgetting what is behind and straining toward what is ahead, I press on toward the goal to win the prize for which God has called me heavenward in Christ Jesus. All of us who are mature should take such a view of things" (Philippians 3:13–15). Spiritually, we are to press on toward the goal of maturity in Christ and all that he has for us in terms of heavenly obligations.

The Bible also makes it clear that we are to press forward and grow in terms of earthly obligations because it is a natural part of our learning to be responsible members of a community. Writing to the Thessalonians, the apostle Paul writes, "We worked night and day, laboring and toiling so that we would not be a burden to any of you. We did this, not because we do not have the right to such help, but in order to make ourselves a model for you to follow. For even when we were with you, we gave you this rule: 'If a man will not work, he shall not eat'" (2 Thessalonians 3:8–10).

Brandon is maturing in his spiritual life and in his job, but he is not pressing on toward the goal of growth. He is mired and stuck in an extended adolescence, in which he wishes to have all the freedom and opportunities of adulthood while enjoying the benefit of his father's picking up the slack for him. It is not that Brandon lacks the skill set necessary to make it on his own, and he certainly isn't discouraged about life. Rather, Brandon and Brandon's father simply need some help with boundaries. Brandon needs to learn to engage in the cooperative behavior that allows him to step up and take a growing share of responsibility—responsibility that leads him toward adulthood instead of toward fun and carefree experiences.

Why do adult kids move back home? Some get discouraged because they have tried to make a go of adulthood but have failed at it or found it almost unbearably hard. Others move back home because they've been ill-equipped to make their own choices, solve unknowns, or handle pressure. Still others move back home because they look down the barrel of adult life and simply don't want to take the responsibility; they would rather depend on their parents and enjoy a time of extended childhood.

We have the same goals for all these children: we want them to become self-sufficient adults. But in each situation, we will need to employ a different mix of encouragement, support, training, and good boundaries to help our adult children achieve independence. Essentially, we must continue to parent these adult children—which isn't as strange as it may first appear.

A century ago, it was commonplace to consider middle teenagers "adults" in terms of work and responsibility. As the century unfolded, we developed an idea that adolescence continued through the later teens or even through the early college years. Then, as now, the primary driving force behind the expansion of that adolescent period was economic.

We are now poised for another redefinition of the length of

time in which children need parenting. This time, however, the parenting must occur while the child has achieved some degree of adulthood and independence. In the next chapter, I'll look at how to utilize and develop a specific parenting plan, but for now it's best to examine a few principles that have to do with how and why this parenting of adult children belongs to us.

Three Principles to Bear in Mind as We Raise Adult Children

No matter why adult children move back home, it is not something to be dreaded or avoided. It certainly isn't a sign of failure — our children's or our own. It is simply a sign that times have changed, and it is now up to our children and to us to make the most of the situation.

On the positive side, it's an opportunity for us parents to utilize a new set of parenting skills. It gives us a second chance to work with our offspring constructively in making an overt difference in their lives. The *goal* of parenting hasn't changed: to raise independent and wise children who are free to participate in the work and family that God has for each of them.

But how do you raise an adult child as compared to a younger child or adolescent? In my experience, I've found three principles to be helpful.

PRINCIPLE 1: Responsibility

An undeniable thread of responsibility runs through parenting. "Train a child in the way he should go, and when he is old he will not turn from it," writes Solomon (Proverbs 22:6). Parents carry the obligation to discipline (23:13), instruct, and teach (1:8; 4:1 – 2). This responsibility, taught throughout the Bible, flows from one generation to the next. All are to prepare children for living life and serving God. As such, much of parenting has to do with tending to the practical demands of daily living, as well as helping to strengthen emotional and spiritual connection to God. Few boomers would ever challenge the idea of responsibility for children; the problem arises when we talk about how long that responsibility continues.

Our culture seems to prefer the idea that once a person achieves adulthood, he or she becomes essentially a peer with his or her parent. In my own field of marriage and family therapy, many have carried this idea to an extreme — believing it is best to begin calling a parent by his or her first name as a signal that parent and child are on the same level. While I can appreciate the idea that as adults we become responsible for ourselves, nowhere in Scripture do I find the idea that our parent ever ceases to be our parent. The truth is that while we become responsible for ourselves, our parents have unique information and training we still need.

Jacob and Esau, for instance, both desired and coveted their father's blessing (see Genesis 27). Parents are able to teach us about what is important in life — though admittedly it is sometimes communicated through the reality that they've lived unsuccessfully or dysfunctionally. At a minimum, our parents usually precede us in the experience of life, thus teaching us about what it's like to lose strength and power and eventually grow old and die. We may be adults, but we can and do still learn from the instruction and example of our parents.

In fact, our parents remain our parents until their deaths. Just so, we remain the parents of our children always. We do not resign from the job of parenting, and we never get a certificate of completion for the job.

In the story of Eli and his wicked sons Hophni and Phinehas, we get a glimpse of how this parental responsibility continues into adulthood. Even though Eli was advanced in age and his sons were adults, Eli had no hesitation in correcting their behavior:

> Now Eli, who was very old, heard about everything his sons were doing to all Israel and how they slept with the women who served at the entrance to the Tent of Meeting. So he said to them, "Why do you do such things? I hear from all the people about these wicked deeds of yours. No, my sons; it is not a good report that I hear spreading among the LORD's people."
>
> 1 Samuel 2:22–24

If you think that Eli was inappropriately butting into his sons' business, God made it clear that this elderly father bore some responsibility for the wicked conduct of his sons:

> "Those who honor me I will honor, but those who despise me will be disdained. The time is coming when I will cut short your strength and the strength of your father's house, so that there will not be an old man in your family line and you will see distress in my dwelling."
>
> 1 Samuel 2:30–32

Even in the New Testament, elders in the church are to be men "whose children believe and are not open to the charge of being wild and disobedient" (Titus 1:6). There is no time limit on parenting, which means we carry some responsibility for our children even after they are able to fend for themselves.

The secret is to understand what sort of obligation this responsibility of parenting translates into. In healthy human development, we think of three things necessary for raising capable and competent children. When a child is very young, we must infuse the child with love and nurture, which provides the child with a healthy sense of self. Loving a child teaches him or her that he or she is precious, worthy of sacrifice, and a joy to have as a companion. Children who experience this kind of love become *confident*. Although we love our children forever, the intense phase of this infusing usually takes place between birth and approximately age six.

We certainly continue to love our children after they reach age six, but our focus shifts to helping them learn responsible limits. We teach them about rules of life and society—such as failing to obey results in unpleasant consequences. We start out in simple terms: "If you don't eat your peas, you won't get dessert." Soon we expand to more complex situations: "You need to be kind and respectful to people, or people will be mean and harsh to you." At this stage of life, children learn about expected behavior and the consequences of failing to follow through on the behavior. Children who have these kinds of expectations and consequences become *cooperative*. Although such teaching and training continue throughout life, parents usually focus on the process most intensely when their children are between ages six and eleven. Before that time, children have a hard time focusing on relationships outside of themselves, and after that time, society usually sets expectations and enforces consequences.

The third element in training healthy children is to help them become self-governing and responsible for themselves. This entails using the child's existing confidence and cooperative behavior to take more and more responsibility in adultlike activities. Instead of working with the child on homework or checking up on whether homework is done, the parent leaves the responsibility and consequence to the child. Instead of asking for an accounting of money, the parent allows the child to govern his or her own resources. As the child ages, he or she is exposed to a growing spectrum of responsibility and freedom. Children exposed to this transfer of responsibility become *independent*. Typically we've thought of this period as lasting from about ages twelve to eighteen. As our society has changed, however, we now understand that at least half of our children will need to experience this transfer of responsibility during an additional six to ten years. This is where the bulk of our responsibility rests.

I'm not issuing a call for us to redo the job of parenting – most boomers have done a more than adequate job in helping their children gain a healthy self-confidence, and have set appropriate limits to teach them cooperative behavior. But the preparation and planning necessary for becoming independent have changed greatly. We must take the responsibility to help our children learn these necessary launching skills in a way that collaborates with them as adults and doesn't infantilize them as small children. We do have a responsibility as parents of adult children, but it lies primarily in helping them leave home and make connections to an independent life.

In practical terms, we're always concerned about our children and their well-being. We always encourage them in their relationship with God and the lessons life is teaching them. We try to be thoughtful and instructive when practical questions arise about how to solve problems, and we make our resources available when our adult children have a responsible, adult plan about how to make progress toward the goal of adulthood. How long do our obligations and responsibilities last? As long as it takes for our children to establish themselves into the work and family life that God has intended for them.

PRINCIPLE 2: Patience

"I can tell you that I will never have a child that returns home for more than a visit," John confidently proclaimed to his group of friends. "These kids who come back home just need a good boot on their backsides to get them into the real world. If parents don't allow them to come back, they'll make it by themselves just fine."

Although we can certainly understand where John gets his attitude – and there *is* something "earthy" about his wisdom – the reality played out very differently with his daughter, Joni.

"Since my dad had made it clear that I could never return home, I really felt trapped," she said. "I had worked hard in school and had a teaching certificate but couldn't get a job my first year out. I tried working as a substitute and took a night job, just to try to make ends meet with my living expenses and loan payments. It finally became too much for me, and I started sinking into depression. Soon I couldn't work and couldn't get out of bed. I was evicted from my apartment, and my credit was ruined from not making payments on time."

When John discovered how desperate and depressed his daughter was, he did agree to take her into his house and help her recover. The damage from the seven months that Joni had been out on her own, however, had some serious consequences not only for her health but also her future financial security.

Certainly John loved his daughter, as evidenced by his willingness to help her after discovering how much trouble she was in; but how had he gotten to the point of so boldly proclaiming that none of his children would ever move home? Whether we like it or not, most of us boomers tie at least a good part of our self-esteem to how well our children perform. It is as if we say, "If my child does well and is successful, then I am a good parent and I'm OK." John belonged to this group. He believed that as long as his child launched successfully out of his house and had become independent and confident, he had measured up as a parent.

We cannot afford to make the mistake of assuming that all adult children should launch at a set time. We have to give up the measuring stick to judge whether we have performed our job of parenting successfully. The goal of helping our children achieve the independence and wisdom that allows them to freely participate in the work and family life that God has chosen for them has no time limit. The process may happen when they graduate from high school, leave for college, graduate from college – or it may happen a decade after college. The reality is that we must learn to work together with them to help them get the right combination of job, relationships, and circumstances that will allow them to get grounded. The method cannot be prescribed, and it takes a tremendous amount of patience – patience with our adult children as they learn how to make the hard choices required to finish the job of growing up and patience with ourselves as we give up old ideas of what makes for a good parent.

It isn't always easy to heed James's advice: "Be patient, then, brothers, until the Lord's coming. See how the farmer waits for the land to yield its valuable crop and how patient he is for the autumn and spring rains. You too, be patient and stand firm, because the Lord's coming is near" (James 5:7–8).

Any of several definitions of patience may be appropriate when talking about adult children moving home, but I believe that James concentrates on what we need the most. He speaks of being willing to wait until the time is right and appropriate – the willingness to utilize all resources at hand and watch how they can work together in order to yield a healthy crop.

When adult children move back home, they certainly don't want to be treated as children, having to put up with curfews and deadlines. They have talents that God has cultivated through years under our roofs. They have skills at planning, anticipating, working, initiating, and developing. They may not be able to get out on their own quite yet, but they want to put to work these skills and talents as they learn how to gain the full independence of adulthood.

Sometimes they will fail in much the same ways we failed when we were younger. But when most of us failed in our young adulthood, we were not in the presence of our parents, and so we gathered ourselves and moved on to the next task. Our adult children often experience these failures in front of us, where we're tempted either to lecture them, as if they didn't know they had just failed, or to take over to try to ensure their success. It takes patience to help an adult child use his or her skills and talents.

John, for example, initially was tempted to take over for Joni and talk to several school administrators whom he suspected might be able to get her a teaching job. "Even though Joni is depressed and has had a rough go of it," I told him, "she really has demonstrated some remarkable skills. She was able to get a degree and then was willing to take two jobs to try to turn things around. She is a hard worker—and you don't want to rob her of the opportunity of landing her own job."

John remained patient while Joni recovered. After she began feeling better, he offered his help by saying, "You've learned a lot through this process. You know how much work it takes to make it, and you also know more about how much you can take. Since you have that knowledge, tell me how your mother and I can be of the most help."

Joni didn't respond immediately, but she did get the clear message that her father had abandoned his strict expectation that she couldn't stay with them as an adult. But she also got the message that her father was confident she could find her way into a job that would be good for her. John shifted from seeing his daughter's depression as his failure into believing it would just take Joni more time to get where she wanted to be. John's exercise of patience gave Joni the support she needed, and she worked with her father to set up interviews that eventually led to a job. But John had to learn that he could not "order" Joni to do anything or manipulate her into doing things just for him.

Joni had to learn that she had limits and needed to protect herself from becoming overwhelmed.

Although Joni did well at her job, she didn't move out immediately but spent another year in her parents' home to get completely out of debt. Doing so helped her take a valuable step toward ensuring she would eventually maintain her independence but also required John to exercise more patience.

PRINCIPLE 3: Boundaries

I've been careful to point out that we boomers never get rid of our responsibility to be parents to our children and that we have to be patient with the amount of time, energy, and experience it may take for them to leave home for good. But note a counterbalance to this responsibility and patience: our adult children are *adults*. Adulthood means they are responsible for the choices they make and therefore are entitled to experience the consequences of those choices. Not even a parent is authorized to exempt them from experiencing the consequences of their decisions.

As we've seen, boomer parents are notorious for their speed and reliability in saving their children from the consequences of their behavior. Stories abound of boomer parents intervening with law enforcement in order to protect their children from "minor in possession" charges, going over the heads of teachers or administrators to appeal to school board members to make sure their children get special advantages or get bad grades "fixed," or perhaps calling in favors or exerting influence to get them places on athletic teams, jobs, or memberships in clubs. All this boomer effort has translated into the twixter generation's believing they have permission, and sometimes a right, to do exactly as they please and still have everything turn out right in the end. The problem, of course, is that this scenario tends to keep the twixters "kids" instead of "adult kids" who are responsible for themselves.

How do we boomer parents make the distinction between our children and our adult children? Put simply, we must utilize proper boundaries with our adult children. By "boundaries" I mean making sure we don't take responsibility for the consequences produced by the adult child. It is the same philosophy I referred to earlier when describing children's needs in terms of normal, healthy development between the ages of six and eleven. During this time, they need clear expectations, with consequences spelled out in case of failure to meet clearly stated obligations. This teaches them cooperation and, more broadly, responsibility for themselves.

The difference between "then" and "now" is that when our children were young, we parents set the expectations and enforced the consequences. But when adult children return home, they are fully adult, and by and large, society in general sets the expectations and enforces the consequences. As parents, we have to be willing to set boundaries around these children to allow them to experience the full brunt of the consequences of their behavior without intervening to "save" them.

I can find no better example in Scripture than the story of the lost son. The younger son insisted that his father give him his share of the estate. Although the son wasn't yet entitled to the money — he shouldn't have received it until the father's death — he did have an eventual claim. The father did not try to talk the son out of such action, withhold the inheritance, or even chastise the son for his impertinence. The father clearly knew the boundary: "You are an adult son of mine, and you can make this decision if you so choose." Certainly the father didn't think it was a good idea; he probably knew his son was ill-equipped to manage such a fortune. But he also recognized that the choice lay with his adult child.

When the son foolishly squandered his wealth in carousing, he suffered the harsh consequences of his foolishness: "After he had spent everything, there was a severe famine in that whole country, and he began to be in need. So he went and hired himself out to a citizen of that country, who sent him to his fields to feed pigs. He longed to fill his stomach with the pods that the pigs were eating, but no one gave him anything" (Luke 15:14 – 16). No one was there to save him, and the son had to experience the consequences of his stupid actions.

Eventually the son came to his senses and developed a plan to get himself out of his mess. He decided to go to his father, confess his sinful behavior, and propose that he become a workman for his father so that he might be kept from starving. So he traveled home. Before he could reach the house, his father spotted him and ran to embrace him. He celebrated his son's coming to his senses. He told the boy's older brother, "We had to celebrate and be glad, because this brother of yours was dead and is alive again; he was lost and is found" (Luke 15:32). Notice what the father did *not* say. He didn't say the foolish brother would now get half of the remaining estate. He didn't even say he had rejected the son's own plan to become a workman. In other words, the father didn't save him from making the wrong decisions in the first place, and he showed no sign of saving him from the consequences of a lost inheritance. The father held these boundaries in place, and the adult son had to run into the wall of the consequences erected by his irresponsibility.

But there is another side of the boundary. Clearly the father believed and knew that his son was still his child. He was overjoyed at the sight of his wandering son returning from his life of debauchery. He loved his son and ran to greet him. He clothed him and gave him a ring to signify that he had not been disowned and counted as dead. He celebrated with the whole community the return of his son. The father wasn't afraid to count the son as his own; he loved him as only a father could love a son and celebrated his homecoming as a special occasion. The son was still his son. It was a clear boundary that the father would always love and be the parent of the son.

In the same way, the boundary we use to balance our responsibility and patience with our children makes sure our adult kids take responsibility for their choices by experiencing the full impact of the consequences of their actions. But this boundary should never include disowning adult children who make unhealthy or unwise choices. We can and should protect ourselves from the irresponsibility of our adult children. If an adult child is a drug addict, for instance, it is perfectly reasonable to protect our household goods from theft and our houses from becoming havens for illegal drug activity. But we can follow the example of the father of the lost son and not refuse to have anything to do with the adult child or deny that he or she belonged to us. We *would* protect ourselves and our property; we *would not* take responsibility for the adult child's consequences; and we *would* continue to love and engage our adult child. By doing so, we follow the principle of boundaries as we raise our adult children.

For us boomers, more than anything else, boundaries mean we learn to let our adult children make their choices and allow them to experience negative consequences without "saving" them. In a similar way to what happens in the ages-six-to-eleven stage, so here the experience of consequences teaches adult kids cooperative behavior and how to be responsible for themselves. This learning often comes at great cost, because the consequences come in full force through "the school of hard knocks." But it is the God-ordained way by which the adult child learns. Practically, it means we boomer parents don't pay off our child's credit card debt or intervene and try to mediate misunderstandings or bad relationships. It means we don't go out and secure opportunities and jobs for our offspring, and it certainly means we don't solve our adult children's problems by giving them money. To be able to execute a reasonable plan for raising adult children, we need to keep in mind the principles and balance of responsibility, patience, and boundaries.

5

CREATING
A PARENTING PLAN
FOR EXIT

My friend, the father of a ten- and seven-year-old, was a committed runner who planned yearly pilgrimages to different cities to participate in half-marathon runs. When scheduling difficulties made it impossible for him to participate in one of his favorite races, his wife suggested that he run his own course through the neighborhoods around his home. His children enthusiastically chimed in that they could help by riding their bicycles alongside to give him encouragement and pacing.

After my friend completed half of his run, his seven-year-old son accompanied him on miles eight through eleven. His son chatted with him a bit, pedaling and talking as his dad pounded out step after step. But after mile nine, my friend started to tire badly.

"Son," he said, "you are going to have to encourage me some. I'm tired and don't know how much farther I can go and how long I can hold on."

My friend's son didn't respond but just continued to pedal

ahead, with his eyes on the road. Finally, after about thirty seconds, the young boy said, "Dad, I got nothin'."

Many times we feel just like this little boy. Our grown children move back home, often deeply discouraged and disheartened, and look to us to say something encouraging to them. But we have things that weigh on us also. First, we have our own lives to manage, with the demands of our marriages and other relationships, as well as holding down full-time jobs. Second, we may well have a parent for whom we're providing (or will be) an increasing level of care. Finally, we see our dreams of winning a certain amount of freedom from responsibility disappearing before our eyes. Our elderly parents and adult children look to us for something that will encourage them. It is a great temptation simply to look at them and mutter, "I got nothin'."

But remember, we never have the option of not being a parent to our adult children. We have something our adult children need—and it is not our money. We have the wisdom, expertise, and fortitude to help our adult children become successful at establishing themselves as independent adults. If our adult kids are stuck—unable to take the next step into adult living—then we should have "something" to equip them to take the next step. What, then, is the exit plan for guiding our adult children toward independent adult living?

INITIATIVE 1: Make and Work a Plan

In order to succeed in helping adult children move toward independence, we must keep in mind—and hold in balance—the three principles of responsibility, patience, and boundaries, especially as we implement this first initiative, namely, *making and working a plan.*

Jesus pointed to the common sense of having a plan for any endeavor when he spoke about counting the cost of being a disciple: "Suppose one of you wants to build a tower. Will he not first sit down and estimate the cost to see if he has enough money to complete it? For if he lays the foundation and is not able to finish it, everyone who sees it will ridicule him, saying, 'This fellow began to build and was not able to finish'" (Luke 14:28 – 30). To have an adult child move back home and stay there for any significant length of time is asking for problems and misunderstandings. An effective exit plan will lay out specifics of who is responsible to execute what action, a reasonable time period in which to complete each action item, and the consequences that will result if the plan is not executed.

Adult children seldom move back already equipped with a plan. They usually see home as a place of safety and a haven where they can regroup and recharge. Many are very discouraged because they've failed to enter the workforce, to form good relationships, or to achieve independence. Many lack the skills, emotional savvy, or problem-solving know-how to be able to move out on their own. Some want to use time at home to have fun, be free, and experience some of the "good life" before settling into a job and family responsibilities. No matter what the situation, the adult child must have a plan for becoming an independent adult.

Because adult children often move back home for an opportunity to be safe and to relax without pressure, the great temptation of boomer parents is to wait and see what their adult child has in mind. Often this "wait and see" turns from days to weeks to months without any sense of how long the adult child will stay and what he or she is doing to make progress toward independence. While there may be value in contemplation and rest, I do not believe this is a reasonable goal for adult children who move back home. The adult child is an adult, and he or she must have the responsibility that goes with such a status.

A difficult but necessary first step when an adult child moves back home is to request a plan from the child within the first few days of returning home. You aren't looking to be hard on your adult child, but it is essential to keep in mind the overall goal of what this stage of raising a child means. Your home is not to be a sanctuary where the adult child can hide from the real world. Being adult means you have to deal with adult ideas, details, and pressures. If you ever doubt whether it's wise to request this plan, remember that it's unlikely *you* can just check out of your responsibilities and move in with someone who will take care of you, nurture you, and feed you. Adult kids who move back home must know from the beginning that, even though they move under your roof, they are responsible adults who are learning to move toward independence. The idea is not to pressure the adult child but to clarify the purpose of moving home — to get equipped to move back out.

Making a plan should first address *the problem that resulted in the adult child moving back home.* Consider Jullian's story. He was a talented student whose interests centered in anthropology and philosophy. While these are noble fields, he was qualified for few jobs after graduating with a degree in those subjects. With no job, he moved back home and did odd jobs and worked as a substitute teacher. These jobs were leading him nowhere, and there seemed little hope of moving toward any form of independence. Jullian's plan had to involve specific training or a change of direction that would put him on a course toward independence. Jullian eventually came up with two plans. The first was focused on learning the trade of carpentry, one he found particularly fulfilling. He found a cabinetmaker who agreed to take him on as an apprentice. The second plan called for him to pursue a doctoral program in anthropology to become qualified to teach at a university. Each plan contained specific details about the amount of time the training would take, the costs involved with each plan, and some of the benefits and drawbacks of each—with the recognition that each detail was important in moving him toward independence.

Another major reason adult children return home is that they've become entangled in a financial mess. With the cost of living so high and wages having gone down, it is little wonder that adult children often have trouble maintaining their independence. A plan to address the indebtedness of an adult child should include calculating whether the child has tried to consolidate loans and negotiate lower rates, whether there is extra income potential to be applied to the debt regularly, and how long it will take to stabilize or eliminate the debt. Again, this plan should specifically address the problem that has made it impossible for the child to gain or maintain independence. Keeping the plan focused on independence prevents both the adult child and the parents from pursuing unfruitful or unattainable objectives.

Second, a plan should spell out *the issues related to responsibility between the parent and adult child.* The focus of responsibility should clearly rest with the adult child, but the plan should also address the assistance that the adult child wants from the parent. Remember Julie's story in chapter 4? Julie was extraordinarily bright. She was an outstanding student and a good athlete in high school. But in college, she just scraped by and returned home when she no longer thought she was making progress toward a degree. Julie was ill-equipped in terms of preparation for independence. Her plan involved learning important lessons about what it takes to pay her own bills, discover her own passions, and take responsibility for herself.

Starting with the idea that any degree was better than no degree, Julie planned to enroll in a general studies program at a nearby university. In addition, she planned to get a part-time job to provide the necessary resources to pay for her car insurance, clothes, and social life. Finally, the plan called for her to take a battery of vocational interest tests to help her find a life direction. Julie was responsible to execute all these elements of the plan, but the plan also asked for specific help from her parents — paying for college tuition, helping her gain budgeting and financial planning skills, and paying for vocational testing. The plan should explicitly detail what is being asked of the parents, how much it will cost, and the time frame by which the tasks should be completed. Julie's plan clearly outlined the things she would have to do to complete her education and learn some life skills but also specifically laid out what would be required of her parents to make the plan work.

Third, every plan should have *specific target periods when each part of the plan is to be implemented*, as well as the time frame for completion of the plan. In this way, both the adult child and parents know whether the plan is fulfilling its purpose and everything is on track for the child to achieve independence.

Fourth, the plan should address *the consequences if the plan gets jettisoned*. Dealing with this issue is particularly difficult for both the adult child and the parents. Who decides the consequences? I'm not talking about minor infractions, such as missing work or not having enough money to pay for a car insurance premium. I'm talking about a significant desertion of the plan, such as dropping out of school or quitting a job with no plans to find another. On major departures from the plan, there *must* be consequences that are distinctly different for an adult child than for an adolescent. In adolescence, the boundary might be something like, "If you don't keep your grades up, I will no longer give you your allowance or pay for your music lessons." Such consequences are totally inappropriate for adult children. With our adolescents, we are still combining discipline with steps toward the child's taking more responsibility. Adults resent discipline, plain and simple. If you want to plant seeds of resentment in your adult child, then draw consequences that remind them of being an adolescent.

Remember that boundaries and consequences for an adult child are taught primarily by society. In society, when we don't perform at a job, we get fired. When we don't make a payment on a car or apartment, the vehicle gets repossessed or we get evicted. In other words, the consequences of the real world are fairly harsh and swift and demand responsibility. When an adult child moves back home, the boundaries and consequences are simple and come down to whether the parent will continue to help and whether the adult child will continue to live at home. If this seems too harsh, keep in mind that the goal of working with an adult child is to get him or her ready to be independent in the real world. In the real world, if you don't show up for work, you get fired. Period.

Here, too, it's important to remember the principle of boundaries. As boomer parents, we should not enforce with anger or disappointment the consequence of asking our children to move out. It does no one any good if we use guilt or manipulation to force adult children into behaving the way we want them to. If we are doing our job as parents of adult children, we have to recognize that they will make their own choices — choices that will sometimes be good and sometimes not so good. If an adult child chooses to deviate from the plan, we don't have to respond with resentment or with the removal of our affection and love. We can simply respect the choice, communicate love and support, reassure the adult child that he or she is always welcome in our home *to visit*, and express a willingness to reconsider future plans of assistance. By displaying this attitude, we communicate that even though parting occurs, the relationship can surely remain intact.

Finally, the plan must be *initiated by the adult child*. The primary reason is that since the adult child is the one with the problems, he or she must be the one to take responsibility to "solve" those problems. If the parent initiates the plan, the parent will essentially be seen as taking responsibility for the plan. The adult child should hammer out the plan and take it to the parents to see if they are willing to help in the way requested. Doing so puts the adult child and parents in a cooperative relationship from the beginning and puts the parents in a position to evaluate whether they think the plan is reasonable and workable — something they can participate in effectively. It puts the parents in the position of evaluators and helpers instead of directors and enforcers. The plan should work much like a partnership between the adult child and the parents.

You may ask, "What if the adult child refuses to come up with a plan or agrees to do so but never comes through?" This is a reasonable question, and it has an obvious answer. Yet again parents must employ the principle of boundaries and tell the adult child that he or she cannot continue living at home. Though loved and welcome to drop in for visits, the child cannot simply hang out indefinitely. Emphasize that if the child needs additional time, training, education, or assistance to "make it" in life, the parents will likely be willing to help; if the child merely wants to be cared for, however, he or she is acting irresponsibly and must learn to live with the consequences.

For several reasons, I suggest that a plan cover a period of no more than two years, except under highly unusual circumstances. First, two years is usually ample time to help an adult child out of a mess or a difficult situation. We're not talking about giving a child an opportunity to have a college experience. These adult children have had such opportunities and now need to get serious about obtaining what they need and moving on with adulthood. Hard work and two years of time can make a huge difference in one's financial situation, and many hours of training can be accumulated in that amount of time. Second, if a plan extends beyond two years, it becomes unwieldy and difficult to manage. Two-year plans can be easily modified and extended if necessary, subject to negotiating between the adult child and the parents. Finally, parents of adult children have other responsibilities and obligations. A parent of an adult child should be willing to have the offspring move back home temporarily but shouldn't be obligated to have that child live at home for an open-ended number of years. In my experience, two years can make significant differences in the lives of adult children who move back home, while longer periods seem to confound plans and work against movement toward independence.

INITIATIVE 2: Offer Help and Safe Harbor

Why do we let our adult children move back home? So we can help them prepare for permanent independence. In other words, *we should want* to provide this help for our adult children as they grow into full adulthood.

I'm a big believer in a plan that helps adult children move toward independence, and I have little tolerance for failing to execute a plan for launching them. But I also know that most adult children who move back home are discouraged or in some type of trouble—or both. The idea of offering safe harbor simply lets our children know that, even though the world is a tough place where they may have had difficulty negotiating the terrain in their first try at independence, home will be a place of safety to get more preparation for the job market, develop practical skills for learning, or work on solutions to some of their problems. I don't believe we should step in and save our children from every consequence the world doles out, and we certainly shouldn't save them from some of the unpleasant realities of life; but those adult children who have been battered by the consequences of the world need a place to retool and repair the damage. We want them to come into a safe harbor to "fix" their problems and right their ships instead of letting them drift and make further poor choices that will only lead to even more complex and difficult consequences.

Such was the case with Edward. Edward seemed to have his life together as a banker who was married to a beautiful woman. He had one son, a two-year-old. But a few years of chasing the American dream had led to a mountain of debt. After four years of marriage, his wife had an affair with another man and informed him that she was taking their son and leaving him. Edward sank lower and lower as he faced the reality of paying the debt he and his wife accumulated, as well as separate spousal maintenance and child support. Although Edward was a Christian, he sought to medicate his pain and discouragement with alcohol. Long nights of drinking soon caused him to miss too much work. He lost his job and his house, and he was on the verge of losing his visitation privileges with his son.

"I was at the lowest I could go," Edward said. "I was drinking too much and was living in a one-room basement apartment. Every personal item I had could fit into a small box."

Edward's father tracked him down and suggested he move back home.

"I thought at first that moving back home at age twenty-eight would be worse than what I was already experiencing," Edward said. "But Mom and Dad both let me know they were making the offer to help me get out of my mess. They didn't give me money or advice; they gave me a place and some space where I could figure things out a bit. Not having to pay rent or buy groceries relieved some of the pressure, but mainly it was having a place of safety where someone else was there to bounce ideas off and to give some advice when I asked for it."

This is the kind of safe harbor most beneficial to adult children. We need to ask for a plan of action, but we also need to give them a safe place that provides breathing room and somewhat limited adult responsibilities. Most of all, we can offer encouragement, patience, and emotional support, knowing it's not easy to make it on one's own.

Some adult children will not return home because they know their parents will judge their actions and not let them forget their mistakes. Jesus cautioned us, "Do not judge, or you too will be judged. For in the same way you judge others, you will be judged, and with the measure you use, it will be measured to you" (Matthew 7:1–2). You may think that since you are fully independent and functioning as an adult, you totally understand what it takes to make it on your own. Though you do know a lot, you don't know what it's like to try to make it just starting out in today's world. If you were in your children's shoes, with their level of experience, you might have made some of the same mistakes they've made. Judging your adult children for bad choices, failures, or false starts is the opposite of the encouraging, patient support they need.

Most boomer parents I meet are eager to offer adult children who move back home a degree of financial support and plenty of advice on how to solve problems. But the safe harbor concept means much more. It says it is ill-advised to offer too much help, especially if it protects adult children from the consequences of their actions. The kind of help I advocate empowers the adult child to solve his or her own problems. It gives the adult child a sanctuary to figure out how to proceed as an adult but refuses to treat him or her like a child, whether by correction or alleviating consequences by cleaning up messes. In this way, the adult child can deal with the consequences in an environment of love and nurture but is still responsible to act as an adult.

Our adult children certainly encounter situations for which they need help, but any financial or training help should be requested by the adult child and incorporated into the plan for independence. Specific help beyond safe harbor and patient encouragement should generally *not* come from the parents. What they really need is our safe harbor, our shelter, so they can move toward making their own adult decisions. Think about this, though: If you find that the consequences of your adult child's behavior are falling more on you than on him or her, or if you find that he or she is using your home to revert to acting more like an adolescent, then you are *not* offering help and safe harbor; you're most likely facilitating his or her irresponsibility.

Edward's parents made it clear that they wanted him to be in a safe place but wouldn't tolerate any drinking. Edward spoke often with his parents about his options but never gave up his prerogative to decide what he should do. He quickly got another job and began digging out of his financial mess by following the principles of a debt management course he had attended. He also participated in counseling to try to reconcile with his wife, although that effort ultimately failed. After fourteen months, Edward found himself divorced – but he had a job, a plan to resolve his debt, and a life that was slowly being put back together. He became more involved with his son and moved out on his own – a much more stable person growing in his ability to maintain his independence.

INITIATIVE 3: Stick to a Limit of Three "Saves"

Many of us boomer parents have been significantly involved with our children from birth through adolescence, remaining connected with our children's successes and probably even more connected with their failures as we tried to correct, train, or resolve wherever appropriate. Therefore we find it extremely difficult to see our adult children fail.

Our adult kids sometimes behave in ways we know will lead

to disaster, such as taking drugs, cohabitating with another person, or involving themselves in risky financial behavior. They make choices that get them in trouble with employers or coworkers, injure church relationships, or put their physical, emotional, or spiritual health at risk. And these destructive behaviors and actions occur both when they're living in our homes and when they're living on their own. So what do we do when our adult child gets in trouble?

One easy answer is to say, "Do nothing unless the child asks for help." In other words, if we believe our adult children must actually behave as adults, we give them the right to succeed or fail on their own. If adult children live on their own, it certainly makes sense to do this, because they will learn from the consequences of those actions (even though it may take a long time and be painful to watch). In other words, if adult children are on their own, they have earned the right to be responsible for their actions.

On the other hand, if adult children are living in our homes, while we have a say in what we will tolerate under our roof, we have little recourse to "make" our adult children do what they refuse to do. In most cases, when they engage in risky or irresponsible behavior, our only remedy may be to require them to move out.

Even though this answer makes sense and is often appropriate, I think there is a scriptural basis for "saving" our children every now and then: "Brothers, if someone is caught in a sin, you who are spiritual should restore him gently. But watch yourself, or you also may be tempted. Carry each other's burdens, and in this way you will fulfill the law of Christ" (Galatians 6:1–2). As the apostle Paul suggests here, we are justified in deciding to swim out to believers in deep water and use our gifts and talents to try to restore them. This is true both for the church family and for us and our adult children. I find the word *gently* particularly interesting as describing how we handle this type of restoration. In my opinion, it doesn't suggest judgment or chastisement but carries the idea of giving a second chance – or as we used to say in our childhood sandlot games, allowing for a "do-over."

There are times when we see a train wreck about to happen in our children's lives. Maybe the wheels already have come off. In that case, we have cause to go to our adult children and give them a second chance, which may mean that in certain circumstances we take some of the consequences for them or "save" them from consequences too painful to bear.

Such was the case for Michelle and her parents, Cindy and Ron. Michelle had moved back home off and on during the first three years after high school. She had begun several vocational programs, such as cosmetology and veterinarian assistant, but lacked the motivation or interest to finish anything. She drifted from job to job, sometimes moving out of her parents' home for a few months but then getting in financial difficulty and moving back. Whether she was in her parents' home or in her own apartment, she acted more like a wild adolescent than anything resembling an adult. Despite her religious faith, Michelle got mildly involved in drugs and became sexually promiscuous. Cindy and Ron felt frustrated and angry, but most of all they worried that their daughter would drift into bigger and bigger problems.

Although Michelle had no plan when she lived at home, her parents did have clear expectations of how she was to behave at home. They insisted that she be respectful of their property and do her share of work. But when Michelle was living on her own, Cindy and Ron felt as though they had little authority to give her advice.

"We were watching anxiously as Michelle was wasting her life," Cindy said.

But then Michelle's life took a serious turn. She began feeling sick and nauseated and lost a significant amount of weight. She would complain about fatigue and feeling achy but assured her father and mother that it was simply a virus that would soon run its course. Cindy and Ron suspected drug use, however, and worried about the impact of her sexual behavior. After consulting with me, they intervened to "save" Michelle. They explained that they wanted her to move home for a while and make an appointment for a complete medical workup. At my urging, they also informed her that they wanted to help her develop a plan to move toward permanent independence — but right now, they were most concerned about her health.

Despite her reluctance, Michelle saw the good sense of her parents' counsel. Good thing, too! The medical workup revealed that Michelle had contracted hepatitis B. For several weeks, Michelle had to be vigorously treated and cared for in order to make progress toward good health. While recovering, she also discovered that she had a sexually transmitted virus.

What if Cindy and Ron had refused to go to Michelle to "save" her? Michelle's condition would very likely have worsened, her reckless behavior would have continued, and she might have quickly spiraled into an even more dismal situation.

We boomer parents may be faced with exactly these kinds of choices. Do we help our child work through the "driving while intoxicated" charge, or do we let him face the consequences by himself? Do we let our daughter default on a loan and let her lose her car and ruin her credit? Do we let our child stay in an abusive or violent relationship with a disturbed partner? Do we stand by and let our children drink themselves into a stupor that may well ruin a career, relationship, or marriage? These are all tough calls. If our goal is to let our adult children simply be adults, then most often we'll let them work out the issues on their own. But I believe God has given us cause to step in at times to stem the tide of disasters in the making. Most of the time, intervening will entail a significant financial and emotional cost to us, and we'll end up shouldering some of the consequences that rightly belong to our adult child.

Of course, there is a balance and a check to everything. If we continually save our children from consequences, they will never learn, grow, and move toward adult independence. While there is a time to save our children, there is also a time to let go, knowing we cannot forever clean up the problems created by adults—and this includes our children. The apostle Paul tells the Corinthians, "I am writing you that you must not associate with anyone who calls himself a brother but is sexually immoral or greedy, an idolater or a slanderer, a drunkard or a swindler" (1 Corinthians 5:11). Paul's teaching does not imply that we stop loving our children or cut off contact from them and treat them as if they don't exist. But it does direct us to find the balance in trying to restore someone who does not want to be restored. And sadly, the time may come when we can no longer help, because our help will only facilitate the irresponsibility of the adult child.

I can't judge whether a parent should help in any given situation; only a parent can make this call. But I do know that repeatedly taking the consequences for an adult child does the parent no good and certainly doesn't help the child in the long run. And so I recommend that once kids are past the age of twenty, parents commit to "saving" their child no more than three times. If you take the consequences for an adult child three times and see that it hasn't helped move him or her toward independent adulthood and responsible behavior, then it is very doubtful that any future protection or saving will do any good. With the limit of three saves, I usually find that boomer parents are much more discerning about stepping in. They tend to make sure that the situation is desperate and serious enough to justify taking the consequences for an adult child, which helps teach the child to take responsibility. The adult child also benefits from the boundary of knowing that there is a limit to what the parents are willing to do.

The idea of sticking to a limit of three saves assures boomer parents that they've done all they can to put their adult children on the right track. Sometimes the saves really do result in the child's using the second chance to become a responsible adult. Sadly, though, I have seen the saves fail much more than they succeed in modifying irresponsible behavior. In Michelle's case, after she recovered from her sickness, almost immediately she failed at implementing the plan she had given to her parents. She once again moved out on her own and soon became a much more serious drug user. Eventually Cindy and Ron intervened once more by sending Michelle to a drug rehab facility—which she left after only thirteen days of treatment. Today Michelle continues her irresponsible lifestyle, with her parents feeling all the pain of not allowing her to move back home and realizing that their daughter remains very much at risk.

After reading the above suggestions and initiatives, you may feel they are clear-cut and rigid. It is important to remember that the goal of working with your adult child who has moved home is to help him or her move toward responsibility as an independent adult. The above ideas are intended to help you make progress in the right direction, but they cannot be applied in simple black-and-white directives. To accomplish the goal it takes patience, understanding, firm boundaries, and grace. In addition, there are a few more things to keep in mind when working with your adult child.

Twixters Are Different

The twixter generation now emerging into adulthood differs significantly from their boomer parents. Twixters have grown up with the expectation that they would be happy, and so happiness is one of the main gauges by which they determine whether life is working out. We boomers also want happiness, but we've learned that the focus of life is *growth* and not mere happiness. Twixters will have to learn this perspective on life, just as we did—and it will be largely up to us to teach them.

Twixters can feel discouraged by unemployment and the prospects that they may never reach the status and living style of their parents. Many of them, therefore, have incorporated a period of unemployment into their plans—we think of them as the *lazy or free-spirited* twixters described in chapter 4. Twixters are highly sensitive to this accusation of being lazy, in much the same way we boomers are highly sensitive to the accusation that we are irresponsible.

Just because a twixter moves home to "experience some fun" or to "relax" for a while, it doesn't necessarily mean the boomer parent should reject the idea outright. Sometimes there are good reasons to take a year out of life to get perspective, enjoy unique experiences, or engage in growth opportunities unavailable down the road once the realities of employment and family come. But if you're going to let your adult child move back home, given this motivation, you should still insist on a clear plan, complete with time limits and consequences. Without a plan, the fun-loving twixter is likely to try to make the "good deal" last as long as possible, which may stretch into several years. If you're going to help one of these free-spirited adult children take time off and have some fun, then I recommend that your plan stipulate that the arrangement lasts no more than one year.

Collaboration Is the Key

An important aspect of learning takes place for adult children moving back home. In truth, they are being trained, corrected, and instructed, with the goal that they become independent adults. Because our adult children are adults, they should be treated as such. Therefore, we don't treat them in ways that suggest they cannot figure things out for themselves. We don't lecture them or use disapproval as a means of discipline. We would not do these things with other adults, and we should not do them with our adult children.

Instead, this model of parenting an adult child calls for *collaboration*. Our adult children have solved problems before, have their own histories of accomplishments, and possess many skills and talents. In many ways, we function with them toward the goal of independence in the same way we function with all believers in the church: "Just as each of us has one body with many members, and these members do not all have the same function, so in Christ we who are many form one body, and each member belongs to all the others. We have different gifts, according to the grace given us" (Romans 12:4–6).

We are not trying to raise our adult children to be us or even to like us; we should desire that they become independent and be their own persons. We must respect their ideas, goals, problem-solving skills, and talents, whether or not we're convinced these things will yield the intended goal. At the same time, we must be careful to ask and expect that our adult children treat us in the same collaborative manner. Our ideas and thoughts are not to be rejected outright simply because they come from us. Both of us should be working on the same team, striving for the same goal of independence.

Paul's admonition to the church should shape this collaborative model between parents and adult children:

Love must be sincere. Hate what is evil; cling to what is good. Be devoted to one another in brotherly love. Honor one another above yourselves. Never be lacking in zeal, but keep your spiritual fervor, serving the Lord. Be joyful in hope, patient in affliction, faithful in prayer. Share with God's people who are in need. Practice hospitality.

Romans 12:9–13

Having said this, when an adult child moves back home, it is still the parents' home. The parents have the prerogative to determine the rules of the house and the requirements the adult child must obey. It is both right and fair for the adult child to have responsibilities in the house, such as cooking meals, doing some cleaning, and helping with some of the maintenance. And it is usually constructive for the adult child to make some kind of financial contribution to the good of the household. But many parents get off track when they start making house rules that resemble those that existed during childhood or adolescence, such as setting curfews, demanding that rooms be cleaned a certain way, or tying financial help to the adult child's performance of some type of action. In general, the rules in a home where an adult child is living should be very few—maybe one or two—and the concentration should be on adult collaboration and cooperation.

Remember Why They Are There

As you and your adult child work on the exit plan, it can be very useful to remember why he or she moved back home in the first place, what emotions he or she had, and what kind of help he or she needed.

A *discouraged* adult child moving back home has typically failed at getting launched into the world. A job setback, financial loss, or relational failure required a move back home. In such cases, the child will feel hopeless, frustrated, angry, and depressed. Boomer parents do well to remember that their primary job is to be patient and to encourage. Being overly directive or demanding regarding the specifics of the exit plan may well crush more life out of the adult child. Give your ideas, express confidence in the child, encourage small steps toward forming the plan, and be patient in the process. This doesn't mean you waffle on the expectation that the adult child either produce a plan or move out, but you realize that the development of the plan will take more discussion and time. Try not to be overly helpful and take too much burden off the twixter! The encouragement and confidence you express, combined with clear boundaries, will eventually result in a plan that will get the adult child up and moving.

Ill-equipped adult children have typically moved home because they've found they don't have what it takes to get a job that will allow them to secure a place and relationships of their own. Again, adult kids in this category will often feel frustrated, angry and hopeless – and they may blame outside circumstances or even you for their inadequate preparation for life. Most of these adult kids will feel rudderless, not knowing what they want to do or wanting something totally unrealistic. They need a little patience and encouragement and a lot of skill training. In many cases, they first need to do the hard work necessary to find their passions or interests – perhaps undergoing a battery of interest testing or going out and working different jobs to get a feel for what they like. (I find it interesting that many ill-equipped adult children typically have had very few or no jobs.) After determining interest or passion, the adult child must formulate direction for a career. If there is a lack of a marketable skill, then he or she will need to outline the necessary training that will lead to eventual employment. In other areas, such as budgeting, managing or organizing life, and being responsible for self, he or she needs to identify ways to get practical instruction. This instruction can come from the parent if the adult child chooses, but it is often more effective for the twixter to get such instruction elsewhere, such as through community service classes or from other adults.

Finally, *lazy or free-spirited* adult children have typically moved home because they want some time to relax or have an agenda that includes having fun. While many of these kids are simply laid-back, a surprising percentage feel anxious about their future and are looking to escape back into an easier, less stressful time. These adult kids need clear boundaries and frameworks that indicate the acceptable amount of time for "resting," with the clear expectation that movement is expected toward independent adulthood.

It's Still Your Life

I've seen many parents make a tragic mistake when an adult child moves back home. They kick into a parental mode and let their goals, dreams, and tasks fall by the wayside.

Having an adult child move back home does require some modifications—living situations, financial obligations, and training—but it should not be an all-consuming job. You should continue to actively develop a deeper relationship with your spouse. Don't feel obligated to spend large blocks of time with your adult child, and certainly don't try to include him or her in everything you do as a couple. This time of life should involve dinners alone with your spouse, weekend getaways, extended travel periods, and vacations—all without your adult child.

Many parents of twixters don't like the idea of an empty nest because they feel they've lost a role with their child. So when the adult child comes back home, they immerse themselves into the old role. Rarely, if ever, does the adult child need or want this attention. If he or she does want this level of attention, then the parents must explain that they need to spend time enhancing their own relationship.

Other boomer parents don't like the empty nest for the very reason that it *does* demand they form a deeper intimacy with their spouse. Many boomers just don't like their spouses enough to want to spend more time with him or her. As a result, if an adult child moves back home, the parents may use the child as an excuse to avoid spousal intimacy—a bad situation indeed that can only produce pressure and unhappiness for the household. If you are having difficulty with your spouse and don't want to spend time developing intimacy, then something is wrong, and it needs to be addressed. Seek counseling or marriage enrichment, but do not use your adult child as an excuse to delay or avoid deepening your intimacy with your spouse.

Some boomer parents neglect their own financial planning when an adult child moves back home. Parents may commit too much of their resources to tend to the goals and desires of the adult child. Other issues and concerns must be taken into account besides the child's financial needs. Boomers have typically either come close to or reached their maximum earning power. Accumulated debts will become increasingly harder to pay off. They also likely will have the added burden of caring for aging parents, which at a minimum will reduce the boomer's ability to earn income and at a maximum will require the boomer to commit a significant portion of income to that care. In addition, many boomers are looking toward retirement, and this time of life is particularly critical in reserving the resources necessary to secure enough funds to last the twenty to thirty years ahead. Finally, boomers want to be free to spend resources on other things, such as on other adult children or grandchildren. Thus the boomer must be careful not to overcommit to providing financial resources or planning time to take care of one adult child. In order to be responsible, the boomer must also plan to manage resources for his or her own needs. It is all well and good to help an adult child financially if necessary, but make sure that the bulk of the financial responsibility and planning rests with him or her.

6

BEING A PARENT AND GRANDPARENT AT THE SAME TIME

The amazing process of multiplication does wonders in evangelism and discipleship. If one believer is faithful to help convert and disciple just one person a year, who will then commit to do the same, the results can stagger the imagination. In just ten years, that lone disciple reproducing himself or herself can result in an astounding 1,024 new and trained believers. Multiplication can produce tremendous good for humanity and the kingdom of God!

But multiplication can also work in the opposite direction, as when things start going south.

Irresponsible action seldom pulls down just one person. When it involves the everyday lives of regular people such as you and me, it can result in broken relationships, debt, poverty, lawlessness, incarceration, and a potential legacy of diminishing resources. Instead of building resources for the kingdom, it moves downward into a vortex of ever-worsening conditions. When resources start becoming scarce, multiplication usually ensures that the hard times will last for years to come.

Adult children typically move back home when they don't have enough resources to make it independently, but there is yet another wildcard out there for many boomers, namely, grandchildren—the young children who accompany the adult child who moves back home.

Grandparents are typically wonderful resources for parents and children. They consistently provide care and both financial and emotional support. In addition, they provide both parents and their children with large servings of fun, security, and wisdom. But about five million grandparents also provide a roof over the heads of their children and grandchildren, financial support for all of their needs, and ongoing nurture and care. In essence, these grandparents become the parents for a complex multigenerational family group where resources can grow scarce. About half of these grandparents will care for both their adult child and grandchildren; the other half will be the sole caregivers for their grandchildren.

In most cases where adult children are present with their children, a relational failure such as divorce is the major cause of the move. In cases where the grandparents are totally responsible for the grandchildren, the move usually followed incarceration of a parent, parental abuse or neglect, substance addiction by a parent, or the disability or death of a parent. In any case, the reason for the move is seldom a positive one—usually a result of tragedy or irresponsibility. Therefore it takes special skill and attention to know how to handle these situations to make sure the process of multiplication results in something good for the grandchildren.

When the Adult Child Moves Home with Children

When your adult child moves home with kids in tow, he or she is usually discouraged, frustrated, and at a very low point emotionally. He or she will often have a load of anxiety — money worries, ambivalence about relationships, concerns about the emotional well-being of the children and about whether things will be OK. The grandchildren typically carry just as much anxiety — separation from a parent, worry about what it will be like to live in an unfamiliar place, and concern about how things will work out.

With so much anxiety around, you may feel tempted to step in and take control of the situation. Grandparents often take total control of the grandkids in order to give the parent relief and time to think through the next moves; what's more, grand-parents sometimes will gravitate toward taking responsibility for their child as they seek to tell him or her what is best or what needs to be done for the good of the children.

As understandable as it is, stepping in really isn't helpful in the long run. Remember, the goal of having adult children move back home is to prepare them for the transition into independent adulthood — and it remains true even if they bring home children. It is better to go slow and make sure everyone takes sound steps to address the living situation of the adult child and his or her children. Make sure your initial decisions build toward the success and good of all. Some of these living situations can last for years, so try to get it right the first time instead of experiencing a string of trial-and-error failures.

STEP ONE: Keep Quiet until the Situation Is Stabilized

I have seen it happen dozens of times. An adult child with children moves in with his or her parents, venting pain and anger. He or she is absolutely determined that the relationship with the spouse is over and that he or she must move on. He or she recites to the boomer parents the litany of complaints about the partner and so stirs the fire of resentment and anger in the boomer parents. The boomer parents get mobilized with this energy, agree with the adult child that the partner is irresponsible and awful—etcetera—and then proceed to tell other people, the grandchildren, and sometimes the estranged partner all the changes that are going to be made to propel the partner out of the situation. With all the focused activity, the boomer parent thinks he or she is on track to have a significant role in helping the adult child move in a different life direction.

But within a week, cracks start appearing in the foundation of the adult child's resolve. The boomer parent finds out that the adult child has been having serious conversations with his or her spouse and that they have decided to reconcile. Not only does the boomer parent have to deal with everything that has been done and said to the adult child and grandchildren; he or she may also have to deal with the awful things said and done to the adult child's partner. The adult child leaves with the grandchildren, and the boomer parent is left feeling confused and isolated, often considered to have been a complicating factor in the rocky relationship between the adult child and partner.

All this to say, be very careful when your adult child moves into your home as a result of relational distress. The adult child may need to vent a lot of things about the frustration that has built up, but realize also that he or she felt attracted to and loved this person enough to commit to a relationship and to have children with him or her. As a result, the anger and frustration can and often does dissipate over time.

Be aware that you do not, and probably should not, have *any* control over the relationships of your adult child. He or she will be involved (or not involved) as he or she sees fit. Be wise, therefore, and keep your mouth closed! You can listen; you can empathize; but keep a rein on your emotions and refuse to become infuriated at your adult child's spouse, because if you do lose control, you may find yourself in a difficult position later on when your adult child decides to reconcile. I know this can be a tall order when extreme circumstances are involved, such as sexual affairs, inappropriate relationships, or violent or abusive behavior—but even then it is best to keep your emotions under control.

When an adult child moves back home because of some kind of relational distress, you'd be wise to look at the move as something temporary. Even if your adult child assures you that the break is permanent, remember that people change their minds. At least for the first week or so, listen to your adult child, help with children and finances when requested to do so, and support the scared and anxious folks under your roof. But be tentative with your actions, advice, and certainly with the things you say about your adult child's spouse. If the separation moves into a second and third week, then it is much more likely that you're looking at a permanent separation; and in that case, plans can begin to be made for having the adult child and his or her children stay under your roof.

STEP TWO: Determine Who Is In Charge

Luke and Lois were in their early sixties when their youngest child, Mica, moved in, along with her four-year-old son and two-year-old daughter. Mica was incensed after discovering that her husband was having an affair and quickly moved to divorce him when he refused to stop seeing the other woman.

Mica's anger often colored the whole day and changed everybody's mood in the household. She would make comments to her children such as, "Your father didn't love us enough to stay with us and chose to go with another woman. We'll be better off without him." She would also say hurtful things to her son such as, "If you don't straighten up, you will turn out to be just like your father."

Luke and Lois knew their daughter was in great pain, but they also knew she was making a big mistake by spouting off such angry and accusatory statements to her kids. Mica's kids were scared and confused about why they weren't living at home any more and why their mother was so angry at their daddy. They soon began throwing tantrums and being aggressive toward one another. Feeling desperate, Luke and Lois tried to suggest to Mica that they were willing to take care of the kids while she got to "feeling better."

"Don't you think I can raise my kids right?" she stormed. "Just give me some space and let me do my job. I don't need you to tell me what I'm doing wrong."

It's difficult to know how to offer help when you encounter such situations. As with all adult children, however, you should treat him or her as an adult. Encourage adult collaboration and cooperation to move him or her back toward independence—especially in the case of the adult child with children in your home, because your adult child must continue to fulfill his or her parenting role.

In order to walk through this labyrinth constructively, you'll want to keep in mind the idea of *hierarchy*. Hierarchy, in this sense, is like an organizational flow chart of a company that shows who is responsible to whom, and who is responsible for what. Your adult child, for better or for worse, is the parent of his or her children. He or she may be terribly inconsistent, too strict or too lenient, overly involved or overly rejecting—but he or she is still the parent and thus responsible to care for and manage the children. Your child must take the responsibility for managing the exercise of discipline, support, care, and nurture.

It is usually unwise for grandparents to step in to "correct" their adult children's parenting skills because it loudly communicates that the adult child is not really in charge. It's similar to what happens when the boss of a middle manager steps in and micromanages an employee who should be supervised at a lower level. The grandchildren who witness such an interaction learn very quickly who is really in charge and therefore who is really responsible. But most of all, this type of stepping in and correcting renders the adult child powerless and adds to his or her discouragement, frustration, and failure.

Adult children should establish the rules for their children, and the children should clearly understand that their parent will enforce consequences and make sure needs are met. Grandparents may still be responsible on occasion for direct care of the grandchildren, but they will provide such care according to the wishes and desires of the adult child. Grandparents can covertly disempower their adult children by refusing to raise grandchildren according to the wishes of the parent or by enforcing a different set of rules when the parent is absent. We may groan when we see our adult children make what we judge to be wrong or bad parenting choices, but it is better to recognize the responsibility of the parent and have him or her deal with the eventual consequences of the bad choices than to take away the power and responsibility, which tends to confuse both the adult child and the grandchildren.

Are there exceptions? Yes. If the parent is under the influence of some substance that impairs decision-making ability, or if the parent is perpetrating any type of abuse or exhibiting violent behavior. In these cases, the potential damage outweighs the problems caused by seizing control and authority.

Remember that you do have a place in the hierarchy. You are the head of the household who has the right to develop and enforce the rules of your own house. For instance, you might want to make sure that there is a general respect for your "things" in the house. You would respect the hierarchy by going to the parent of your grandchildren in private and describing your expectation. You would be open to listen and make modifications.

If the parent has a very young child, for instance, certain fragile things would be better placed out of reach or packed away. The parent and you would work together to determine how best to carry out your expectations and desires and how to make it work in actual practice.

The same principle holds true when you want to give your adult child input on his or her parenting skills. Observers can often see things that those involved in the interaction cannot see—especially when it comes to parenting. In instances where I've had to discipline my children, my wife has often come to me later and suggested that I came across as much too harsh and angry. Even though I usually get defensive, I almost always have to acknowledge that she spotted an area of my parenting skills in which I could improve. The point is that she did not correct me on the spot, in front of my children; instead, she waited until we could evaluate the incident collaboratively and in private. So it should be when you want to help your adult children with parenting. You may have great ideas, but you need to respect the hierarchy and give them the information in private so they have the option of working collaboratively with you. If you correct in front of your grandchildren, you will only anger your adult child and run the risk of teaching your grandchildren that you do not support the parent—a lack of support that will eventually undermine your adult child's authority and eventually his or her responsibility.

When Luke and Lois came to see me, they felt confused and unsure about how to handle Mica's angry outbursts. I explained, "She is the parent and is in control, but you do have a right to expect that the mood in your house will remain constructive and positive."

We brainstormed how they might set a plan in motion in which they would tell Mica that they expected her to keep her outbursts in check or to express them in private or to a counselor. They further expressed that they would support Mica's parenting decisions but would not accept an angry, accusatory tone in the house, because it was bad for everyone in the house. Mica predictably responded with anger, but after she cooled down, she admitted that she knew her parents were correct. A very fruitful conversation then ensued in which Luke and Lois offered to listen to Mica's frustration about her soon-to-be ex-husband, and she would work at pulling the plug on her anger around the children.

You have a place in the hierarchy, but it is as a consultant, not a dictator. Your adult child is the parent and has the power to be the direct decision maker for your grandchildren. Be cautious about undermining his or her authority and power! Cooperate with your adult child to support his or her parenting of the children according to the style and rules desired by him or her. When you are in charge of the children, let them hear you speak as an advocate of the parent's choices, regardless of whether it reflects your own particular parenting style. If you believe certain issues need to be changed, work with the parent in private to suggest and guide toward possible change. If you want to enforce certain house rules, then work with the parent in private to brainstorm how to effectively make sure your desires are respected and implemented. In the same fashion, don't allow yourself to be co-opted into taking the power and responsibility for the grandchildren. If the adult child has children, he or she should be the parent — period. If he or she shirks this responsibility, address the situation in the exit plan to achieve independence.

STEP THREE: Determine a Plan

Adult children who bring children back home to live with you are still adult children who need to move toward independence.

Often, these adult children have been forced to move back into your home because they or their spouses, or both, have been financially irresponsible. In some cases, they are accustomed to having two incomes in the household and find that a potential split has cut earning power in half. In other cases, the adult child has relied on the partner to provide all income for the family, and he or she is ill-equipped to provide for himself or herself and the children. These issues accompany any adult child moving back home, and the problem is complicated by the fact that children increase the emotional needs within and potential expenses of the household.

Even so, the same type of plan discussed in chapter 5 is required — outlining the financial help, additional training or education, and skills that are needed for the adult child to once again be independent. Be clear how the objectives are to be met, as well as the time frame for implementation. In addition, include parenting goals and objectives for each grandchild.

In my opinion, it is essential that the adult child develop the plan for himself or herself, as well as for the children. The adult child should then take the plan to the boomer parents for their decision on whether they are able and willing to provide the support, finances, and care called for by the plan. Negotiation may be required, but try hard to get this plan implemented within the first few weeks of the adult child moving back home. The longer that boomer parents go without a plan, the more likely it is for an unhealthy drift to occur. They must insist that the adult child be responsible, and they must refrain from taking on the adult child's parenting responsibility.

Tammy was typical of many adult children who return home with their own children in tow. Tammy was a believer who had married an unbeliever; together they had a six-year-old son, Caleb. Tammy's husband, an alcoholic, often would erupt in violent outbursts. While he never physically abused Tammy or their son, his emotional abuse prompted Tammy to leave and return home to her mother's house.

Since Tammy had no job skills, Tammy's mother was concerned that her daughter might depend exclusively on her to take care of everything. So she requested a plan from Tammy on how she would proceed toward independence. Tammy proposed that she would take an eighteen-month course in auto mechanics. She would work at an after-school day care center for three hours a day, where Caleb's after-school care would be at no cost. She was confident about her budgeting and financial skills, since she had managed the finances in her now-broken home.

Despite a messy divorce, she had no significant debt. She asked her mother to provide free food and rent, to pay for her car insurance, and to pay child care for Caleb during the two summers she would be in school. Even though her mother had reservations about whether Tammy could make it on what she had requested and the few hours she planned to work, she agreed to the plan and offered to help in the way Tammy suggested.

"Things were very tight for us," Tammy said. "The plan really left me and Caleb very little for any extras. But I felt I was working toward something on my own, even though I was getting help from Mom. It gave me a sense of pride and accomplishment to stick to the plan and make it work."

Tammy did execute the plan and had no trouble getting a job as a mechanic. The fact that she was a female made her a desirable "hire," as females were underrepresented in that profession. The plan served both Tammy and her mother well and kept her goals and objectives on track.

Up to this point, I've focused on situations in which an adult child has moved back home with children after a relational break from a spouse. But it is common these days to deal with an adolescent child who is unwed or unpartnered and has a child. In these cases, it is important to remember that the child who has had a child must make the transition into independent adulthood, even if she has to make that transition in her middle-teen years. The plan, therefore, must be specific with regard to completing education, working, and contributing to the household. Although it will undoubtedly be difficult, the adolescent must make the transition into parenthood. If the boomer parents maintain the expectation that the child will parent, the child usually will transition to the role.

Too often boomer parents make the mistake of excusing their child from the obligations of parenting, believing that he or she needs time to experience their own adolescence. For better or worse, the child *is* a parent, and it will be counterproductive for boomer parents to facilitate a child's adolescence when the child has to be facing up to the reality of parenting. In the case of an adolescent parent, the plan of transition into independent adulthood often takes a bit longer, but it still should be clear on issues of education, work, and financial contribution, with clear time frames spelled out.

STEP FOUR: Determine to Be a Grandparent

If you succeed in keeping your adult child committed to responsible parenting and have a plan in place for progressive independence, then you need to consider that you have another important role to fulfill, namely, that of being a grandparent.

Scripture doesn't make many references to the obligation of grandparenting, but one important principle is implied, reflected in an Old Testament verse such as this one: "Only be careful, and watch yourselves closely so that you do not forget the things your eyes have seen or let them slip from your heart as long as you live. Teach them to your children and to their children after them" (Deuteronomy 4:9). Grandparents have the obligation to pass down godly precepts and wisdom not only to their children but also to their grandchildren.

But teaching and passing along wisdom to grandchildren looks very different from teaching one's own children. We have the primary obligation to tutor and instruct our own children in the basic mechanics of daily living. We teach young children what and how to eat, how to dress, how to behave, and how to keep themselves and their "stuff" clean. As our children grow, we teach them how to work, make responsible decisions, live up to obligations, and be courteous and kind. We also teach principles and wisdom about God and nurture our children emotionally, of course, but with all the practical teaching that goes on, these principles often get pushed to the back burner.

As grandparents, however, we aren't pressed by the obligations of basic instruction, because the parent has the primary duty to teach these things. We should be able to spend quality time with a grandchild and impart pearls of wisdom and emotional security unfettered by the press of homework, activities, and such. Our grandchildren need grandparents who take them special places, just by themselves—to the zoo, to the ice cream shop, or out for a long walk or bike ride. They need to hear stories of our growing-up years—both our successes and failures—that reassure them that life can turn out OK, even in the midst of stressful circumstances. They need to hear from our mouths how absolutely special and precious they are, without being pressed by our urgings to get something done or to arrive at a certain place on time.

And even more important, they need us to listen to their hearts. They need to know they have an adult who will listen to them in a nonjudgmental way and still accept them. Let them know they can bring to you the struggles, questions, and hurts that cannot be heard by parents who themselves are in pain.

Listen to the story of an eighteen-year-old, who recalled

191

the times he spent with his grandparents during his parents' divorce:

"It was my grandparents' house that saved me. The year and a half that my mom and I moved back in with them was one of the toughest I'd ever known. My mom was depressed and could barely pull herself out of bed to go to work. It was like my dad deserted not only my mom but me as well. Both of them were so caught up in what they were doing to each other that they forgot about me. But every time I thought I was on my own and no one really cared about me, my grandparents were always there. My grandmother would be there with a piece of cake, or my grandfather would say, 'Let's go to the ballgame.' They would always acknowledge me and tell me what a good kid I was, and they would reassure me that all the stuff with my parents would pass. They were right—the stuff did pass. Mom went back to school and eventually started an accounting job, and Dad and I have reconnected. But it was my grandparents who held me together when I could have easily come apart at the seams."

If your adult child is living with you, he or she should take the parenting responsibility for your grandchildren. You must be free to do your job as a grandparent, which at its essence is to make sure your grandchildren are infused with the confidence that you and God love them. They need your emotional support and nurture, unattached to any expectation. You need to be free to listen to their hurts and pain and give them the wise assurance that if they keep putting one step in front of the other, they'll see that God is faithful and that things will get better.

Grandchildren most often come to live in the home of grandparents out of situations where there has been severe pain and turmoil. As a grandparent, you can speak to that pain in a way in which no parent can. Free yourself up to do your job.

When the Grandparent Becomes the Parent

As mentioned near the beginning of this chapter, about two and a half million grandparents will have sole responsibility for raising their grandchildren — and the reason is almost never pleasant. In most cases, grandparents become parents when the parent is highly irresponsible and buried under problems. The adult child may have been addicted to some type of illicit substance and has had the children taken away by Child Protective Services. It is often an emotional roller coaster of an experience for both the grandchildren and the grandparents, as the adult child disappears for a period and then suddenly shows up, wanting (or threatening) to take away the children.

Boomer grandparents have myriad understandable emotions when they accept the primary parenting responsibility for their grandchildren. Many feel confused and ill-equipped. As one woman put it, "After all, I have living proof in my daughter that I am an incompetent parent, because I raised her to be a terrible parent and a drug addict." We know we have skills and can offer a better environment than the one provided by our irresponsible adult child, but the thought of our own failure in raising our adult child is often hard to shake.

We may often feel resentful and angry as well. We accomplished our job in raising children, so why should we have to start the process all over again? We may feel cheated, thinking it was supposed to be our time to slow down and enjoy some freedom, but now we're faced with more years of raising children. Finally, many may feel isolated and alienated. Where do grandparents who are still parenting little kids *fit*? Certainly, they find it difficult to fit with people of their own age group who have moved into retirement and are slowing down. In many cases, grandparents get the job when the grandchildren are very young, and so they have years ahead of them of raising school-age children and adolescents. At the same time, they don't fit their "normal" parenting counterparts, who are generally about thirty years younger. This makes for a painful loneliness as the grandparents feel they must bear the job alone with no support.

Match Power and Responsibility

It is very difficult to come to the recognition that our own child is unfit as a parent. We want to believe the best about our children and never give up hope that they will get things together. But when grandchildren end up in our home without parents, we must learn to face the hard facts—that at least for the time being, our child *cannot* be the parent.

Because the alternatives can be costly, time-consuming, and emotionally wrenching, grandparents often take on the job of parenting their grandchildren without any formal agreement or legal grounding. The primary problem here is that without legal authority, grandparents often lack the power to effectively deal with schools, health agencies, and support institutions that require such legal proof of authority. Worse yet, in the absence of any legal grounding, the adult child can return at any time and legally take the child—and the grandparent has no support for maintaining a stable environment, even though the grandparent may have been serving as parent of the child for years.*

Boomer parents faced with raising their grandchildren alone must have the legal standing to do the job effectively. If the parent has proven over time to be unstable and irresponsible, then it is highly likely that the instability will continue for a long time—and that situation certainly is not in the best interest

---

* Some states have passed laws called "consent legislation" in which a parent can give a grandparent legal rights to "parent" the child in the areas of medical assistance or school enrollment. But be advised that the parent of your grandchild can remove this consent at any time.

of your grandchild. It is essential to take the necessary steps to gain the legal standing to take over the parenting job. This will most often mean pursuing custody, guardianship, or adoption.

Custody of a child is a legal mechanism in which the rights of a parent are given to a person who will act in the child's best interest. The person who has the responsibility for custody is typically called a *managing conservator.* In most cases, it is far easier to be assigned as a legal managing conservator of a grandchild than to pursue other courses of action. In most states, a petition must be brought before a judge to change conservatorship of a child from a parent to a grandparent. It is important to note that the law assumes a parent will be the conservator of a child and will most often seek out a biological parent to serve in that role. If the court believes there is good reason that one of the biological parents will not serve in the capacity of conservator in the best interest of the child, then the court is free to assign another managing conservator. In these cases, of course, you or an agency must present information that supports the contention that a biological parent should not be the managing conservator. It is difficult to present such information and evidence against one's own child, but it is a necessary step if you are to have the power to effectively raise your grandchild.

Child Protective Services (CPS) often gets involved in custody cases. In many cases, irresponsible parenting has resulted in abuse or neglect. If you see evidence of this in your grandchildren's lives, you shouldn't hesitate to call CPS in order to protect your grandchildren. It may mean your adult child will be prosecuted for abuse or neglect, but this kind of intervention may be the impetus for getting the help needed to recover or become more responsible. At any rate, it is much too risky to leave grandchildren in abusive or neglectful situations, no matter what the consequences for your adult child. If CPS finds abuse or neglect, the agency will take custody of the children.

In such cases, CPS frequently seeks grandparents or relatives to act as managing conservator, or sometimes assigns the grandparents to be foster parents. Agency help can be useful in this process, but be aware that if CPS finds evidence of abuse or neglect, there will almost certainly be restrictions on your adult child visiting in your home with the children present. You must be willing to adhere to these orders strictly, or CPS will find another location for your grandchildren.

Another legal option is to pursue *guardianship*. This course of action is typically pursued when the biological parents of the grandchild are either deceased or missing and someone needs to have the authority to make major decisions for the child.

In some cases, you may want to pursue *adoption*, which can be difficult because to adopt your grandchild, the parental rights of the biological parents have to be terminated. Although it is much easier and more likely to have a judge rule that it is in the child's best interest to assign a grandparent as a conservator, it is a difficult matter to have a judge terminate a parent's rights. Again, if you pursue this course of action, you must be willing to present evidence about the severe and chronic nature of your child's parental deficiencies, as well as the unlikelihood of your adult child being rehabilitated. This course of action, though undeniably sad, is often necessary to get the authority needed to effectively raise grandchildren.

Why would you ever take custody of your grandchild away from your adult child? Primarily so you can stabilize and protect the grandchild from the intrusions and irresponsibility of the adult child.

Joseph was a nine-year-old boy in a world of trouble. His mother was an alcoholic drug user who had turned to prostitution to get money to feed her addictions. She was totally focused on drugs and had left Joseph to take care of himself. As a result, Joseph could not read or write and had the cognitive functioning of a five-year-old. Worse yet, he was underweight and underdeveloped. Although his grandparents would gladly have taken Joseph in, they had not heard from their daughter in years and had no idea she even had a son.

When Joseph's grandfather finally discovered he had a grandson, he drove to the town where his daughter was staying and searched until he found Joseph. He brought him home with him, and the grandparents faithfully cared for Joseph, enrolled him in a special school, got him medical care, and introduced him to their church community. Joseph responded remarkably. Although he was still small, he gained weight and caught up on much of his development. Within two years, he was within a year of his chronological reading level age. He was making friends and loved his middle school youth program at church.

Then one day his mother showed up. The grandparents insisted she couldn't take Joseph. She returned with a police officer, who asked the grandparents for documentation that would show they had legal custody of the boy. When they couldn't produce anything, the police officer looked at Joseph and said, "Is this your mother, and do you want to go with her now?" To the surprise and shock of the grandparents, Joseph answered, "Yes."

Within a week, Joseph was once again being neglected and had fallen into a terrible situation. Why did he say yes? Because even abused children want to have their parents love them and do all they can to care for them. Even when there is no hope for reform, children hold on to the hope that parents will change.

Legal standing brings stability and holds the grandparent and grandchild together during the unpredictable times of the adult-child intervention. It may be unpleasant and difficult to attain, but gaining legal authority to parent the grandchild is absolutely necessary.

Seek Support

Most grandparents who raise grandchildren on their own find financial and health support difficult to attain. The social support programs in the United States are declining. Many states don't provide adequate health insurance for children who are not covered under an existing policy, and welfare support for grandchildren in the home is limited and temporary. In addition, most states have woefully inadequate support available for housing. Nevertheless, if you are a grandparent raising a grandchild, you need to seek whatever social support is available through the government or the local community.

Who is most likely to take up the cause of a child uncared for by an irresponsible adult who is unable or unwilling to raise the child? Take a bow, grandmother. This grandmother is likely to be over the age of sixty, have health problems of her own, and be on the edge of poverty. She is most likely to be single and often has more than one grandchild in her home. I don't foresee an increase in government resources or a greater ease in accessibility to health and welfare services any time in the near future. So where does one go for support and care? If you are parenting your grandchildren and don't have adequate means to care for that child, seek support from the local church. This may mean you'll need to seek out grandparents in similar situations and form emotional support teams to combat the problems caused by isolation and alienation. You may need to go directly to pastors or church leaders to explain the plight and need of yourself and your grandchild.

It would be easy to say that the church should see the need and offer care with no prodding, but very few churches notice the real needs of this population. Instead, boomers in these situations must present the need to the church. In my experience, when grandparents put flesh and bones on a problem few people even know exists, church members often respond with emotional, financial, and social support. Yes, it's hard to seek support, but it is often best to seek that support from within the church body.

It's a Worthy Job

At first blush, parenting grandchildren alone doesn't look like a fair job. We take on a role we thought was in our past and one in which we feel the jury is still out on how we actually did. While our peers are free to pursue other interests or to slow down a bit, we are charged with gearing up to get children to activities or to help them with homework. We have trouble fitting in, and we wonder if we are doing any good. As a result, many grandparents question whether they should engage in the task. Indeed, many would refuse the task of parenting grandchildren if only somebody else would step up to do the job.

Be assured that the job you do in raising grandchildren makes all the difference in the world. The research clearly shows that children raised by grandparents do much better in life than children raised in foster care homes and significantly better than children raised in traditional single-parent homes. Grandparents, while far from perfect, seem to have learned the lessons of life well, and they exhibit strength and tenacity in raising grandchildren to maturity.

Think of the challenges that most children face when they move in with grandparents. Most have come from backgrounds of neglect and abuse, have grown up around illegal behavior, and have endured living situations that were erratic, undependable, and often dangerous. Yet, grandparents provide stability that gives grandchildren a healthy home and a second chance.

The apostle Paul writes, "Praise be to the God and Father of our Lord Jesus Christ, the Father of compassion and the God of all comfort, who comforts us in all our troubles, so that we can comfort those in any trouble with the comfort we ourselves have received from God" (2 Corinthians 1:3–4). This is what grandparents do as they raise their grandchildren alone. They reach out with compassion and comfort.

Like Jesus who looked to bless those in trouble, so grandparents give to grandchildren the comfort they themselves once received. They often inherit the job of parenting grandchildren as a result of sad and tragic circumstances, but by doing it well, they literally save the lives of their grandchildren. It is a worthy job honorably defined by sacrifice – the kind of sacrifice that Jesus himself was willing to make on behalf of humanity.

PART 3

THE
CHALLENGE
OF

Retirement

7

WE CAN'T ALL BE WAL-MART GREETERS

My wife and I immensely enjoy our (nearly) annual pilgrimage to Laity Lodge, the Howard E. Butts Foundation camp. Nestled in a canyon along the Frio River in Texas hill country, the lodge is a beautiful, quiet retreat center where people can freely seek God's face. One of the unique features of the site is the drive that goes up a section of the hard limestone riverbed. As you drive in the river, it feels as though all the cares of the world wash off your burdened and weary mind. It is one of the great benefits of the terrain—and just one of the many things that makes Laity Lodge so special to us.

But you do have to drive *in* the river, which makes it particularly challenging if it happens to be raining hard on the day you want to leave. We often say, "The Lord willing and if the creek don't rise," but at Laity Lodge, you have to take the saying literally.

On one of our trips, it had poured the night before we were supposed to leave, and the water had crept up a bit. By midmorning, the rain had stopped and the sun had come out in its full splendor, so I assumed we would have no problem leaving in the afternoon.

I was dead wrong.

Remember, the lodge lies at the bottom of a canyon, so all the surrounding land for miles and miles drains into the river. Rain from the immediate area had caused the river to rise slightly the night before, but once the whole confluence of water began rushing in for hundreds of square miles, we had a flash flood on our hands.

So it is with the third major challenge boomers will face – a challenge that will change life forever. For years we've heard of the growing problems with funding for Social Security and Medicare, concerns over underfunded or bankrupt pension programs, the low savings commitment of Americans, and the concerns over reduced benefits from employers. But like my experience in the canyon, everything seems to be functioning OK, so we assume we will get through these problems in reasonably decent shape.

But when the full brunt of baby boomers hits the retirement market, the confluence of these problems and the lack of attention paid to them will begin to hit in full force. We'll have a flash flood on our hands.

We have seen how these problems are already affecting many people who have tried to retire, but by the time it's all said and done, at least a third of us boomers will experience severe financial problems after we retire. The problem is quite simple: there simply won't be enough money or services to supply us with what we need to live in retirement. And so the third piece of the reality puzzle is now in place: *Many of us will retire only to have to go back to work.*

We will be the first Caregiving Generation, not only because we will be caring for our aging parents and our adult children who move back home, but also because we will have to care financially for ourselves in ways we never imagined.

Don't Kid Yourself, the Problems Are Real

The confluence of big problems begins with the population of retirement age. The current stress of the Social Security and Medicare programs is caused not by people *entering* the system but by people who will *not leave* the system. Currently, when men and women reach the usual retirement age of sixty-five, they live on average to be eighty-one and eighty-four, respectively. This is the *average* age, which means that many more adults live long past age eighty-five, when health problems — and the need for long-term care — become most acute.

Simply stated, older people live much longer than their predecessors did, and the government programs for retirees was never intended to handle people for that length of time. As a result, the system labors to pay expenses for the present population, reducing the trust fund capacity for those about to retire. With the system already weakened by a generation that lived longer than expected, the boomer generation will find scarce resources in these already reduced trust funds.

In addition, the boomer generation reaching retirement will be larger than any generation in the nation's history, which simply translates into more people drawing resources from the system. And as if this isn't enough, boomers will live much longer in the system than even their predecessors did. Men will have an average longevity of about eighty-four, while women will likely live to a whopping eighty-eight! Again, these are *average* ages. The boomers will have more people in retirement than any previous generation, and most will live well into their eighties. A huge percentage of them (maybe even a majority) will live into their nineties, and there will be more centenarians than ever before in history.

For the last four censuses, the largest growing age category by percentage has been the group eighty-five and older, and this trend will certainly continue through the first half of this century. This flood of the retired population will stress retirement resources to the maximum; it is the first confluence of retirement woes.

And it is not merely the government trust programs that this retired population explosion will affect; it will also influence private pension programs. At least with the government trust program, funding is continual from the present generation. Many companies, whether through mismanagement, fraud, or default, failed to fund their pension programs adequately (or at all). Think back to companies such as Enron. Many people pinned their retirement hopes on programs heavily invested in their stock and pensions. Many lost most of their retirement capabilities, and most lost more than they can ever hope to recover. Many of these companies have simply given up on their pension responsibilities and promises and defaulted on their obligations. As mentioned in the introduction, the government does have a pension insurance program for these companies – the Pension Benefit Guarantee Corporation (PBGC), but the government never anticipated the sheer number of companies that would default. The PBGC is underfunded and stretched to the limit. Already it will pay only dimes on the dollar, and as the century progresses and more companies default, it is likely that even less money will be paid out to pensioners.

This isn't simply a problem of government and corporation trust funds. Many companies have tried to solve their "retirement woes" by moving workers to 401(k) plans, in which the company will match an equal percentage of the employee's contribution, up to a maximum amount. But Americans have never

saved less in the nation's history, and so they chronically under-
fund their own retirement plans. Certainly this will affect the
younger generations more than boomers, but many boomers
also have these 401(k)s in place and haven't funded them properly. And many people lack the business know-how to properly
invest and get a reasonable rate of return on their retirement
investments, which further complicates the issue of adequate
funds for retirement. What's more, divorce and unemployment
have diminished the boomer generation's ability to save money
and put away resources for retirement. This is the second confluence of retirement woes, namely, *pension and retirement funds are
severely underfunded.*

Of course, government programs such as Social Security and
Medicare face these funding problems also. As the obligations
of the trust fund grow, the resources will shrink, unless future
workers make substantially larger contributions. The problem
is that there will be far fewer workers as compared to the aging
population. In 2000, there were 4.8 people aged twenty to sixty-
four in the labor force as compared to each person sixty-five and
older. By 2030, experts project that the ratio will be only 2.9
people in the labor force to one person of retirement age. The
lower birthrate of post-boomers has translated into a shrinking
labor pool when compared to the burgeoning retirement population. Fewer workers means less money contributed into "pay
as you go" retirement trust funds such as Social Security and
Medicare, and so the contribution dollars for boomer retirees
will simply dry up. This is the third confluence of retirement
problems, namely, a shrinking labor force will mean *fewer contributions into already overburdened retirement trust funds.*

Don't kid yourself—the clouds already have burst and the
waters are pouring in from these multiple sources, creating
a "flash flood" of retirement disaster. Very simply, too many
people will be seeking too few resources from too few people

with the ability to help. It is not a matter of when this will happen, because the problems already have begun to appear. All we're doing now is waiting for the deluge to converge at the bottom of the canyon—a convergence that will take place between 2010 and 2040.

By no means am I am predicting the end of the world, because after 2040, the outlook is much brighter. But I am saying that this will spell the end for retirement as our parents knew it. With fewer resources available, boomers will simply have to find additional resources.

If you feel overwhelmed by all this information, don't worry—you're normal. But like the issues of aging parents and adult children moving back home, this one is simply too pressing to ignore. Don't be like the foolish person who built his house on the sand: "The rain came down, the streams rose, and the winds blew and beat against that house, and it fell with a great crash" (Matthew 7:27). Some issues you simply cannot deny or ignore and still hope to be OK. You must be wise and prudent, like those who follow the good sense reflected in this verse: "The heart of the wise inclines to the right, but the heart of the fool to the left. Even as he walks along the road, the fool lacks sense and shows everyone how stupid he is" (Ecclesiastes 10:2–3).

Both the Bible and social consciousness demand that we plan and prepare well for what is ahead. Therefore, we must take an honest look at how we will learn to cope with the coming stresses.

Surviving the Flood

How are we going to make it through the retirement flood in which there will be too many demands and too few resources? Let's first consider the idea of working versus retirement.

The American Association of Retired People tells us that almost 80 percent of us expect to do some type of work when we retire. This is a good thing, because many of us will *have* to be employed to make ends meet. But what kind of work will we do? After all, there are so many of us boomers. We can't all be Wal-Mart greeters.

Retirement: Is It Biblical?

It is a fair question to examine the whole idea of retirement. The Bible makes it clear that God intended humans to work as part of what it means to live in his kingdom. Many people mistakenly believe that work was a punishment associated with the fall of humanity when Adam sinned. But such is not the case.

Long before the fall, it is written of Adam and Eve, "God blessed them and said to them, 'Be fruitful and increase in number; fill the earth and subdue it. Rule over the fish of the sea and the birds of the air and over every living creature that moves on the ground" (Genesis 1:28). God gave humanity a command to bring organization out of the material of creation, which entails work. This organization ties us in with God's creative, productive, and procreative nature.

The account continues: "Then God said, 'I give you every seed-bearing plant on the face of the whole earth and every tree that has fruit with seed in it. They will be yours for food. And to all the beasts of the earth and all the birds of the air and all the creatures that move on the ground – everything that has the breath of life in it – I give every green plant for food" (Genesis 1:29 – 30). God also gave work to humanity to provide for human need. Work is meant to bring organization out of a messy world and to help us utilize what is available to meet our needs. God inspired work; it was a part of his plan from the beginning. In fact, the second chapter of Genesis makes this idea explicit: "The LORD God took the man and put him in the Garden of Eden to work it and take care of it" (Genesis 2:15).

But there is every indication that the fall did change the *nature* of human work:

To Adam [God] said, "Because you listened to your wife and ate from the tree about which I commanded you, 'You must not eat of it,'

"Cursed is the ground because of you;
    through painful toil you will eat of it
    all the days of your life.
It will produce thorns and thistles for you,
    and you will eat the plants of the field.
By the sweat of your brow
    you will eat your food
until you return to the ground,
    since from it you were taken;
for dust you are
    and to dust you will return."

Genesis 3:17 – 19

After the fall, the nature of work became unpleasant, burdensome, and much harder. But the original idea of work – to bring organization and to provide for human need – remains the same.

Where did we get the idea of retirement? Until recently, retirement was quite unlikely. People simply worked up until their death, or if they were unable to work, they relied on the support of family or friends. But in the late nineteenth and early twentieth centuries, nations begin providing some type of pension for retirement in old age, and then as the twentieth century progressed, employers started taking over the task of providing retirement money. It is a concept limited almost entirely to industrialized countries, because only these places have the resources to enable people to retire.

And the retirement age differs greatly from country to country. For instance, in France you can retire after age fifty if you have worked for at least thirty years. In most countries, the retirement age is somewhere between ages fifty-five and seventy. In the United States, we normally think of retirement at age sixty-five, although that age will creep up to age sixty-seven over the next several years. Mandatory retirement in the United States for Social Security is age seventy. And there are exceptional kinds of retirement. Generally, the more laborious, taxing, or dangerous the job, the earlier the retirement age; for instance, the military usually allows retirement after twenty years of service.

The original idea of retirement referred to the time when a man no longer had the ability or strength to work; it was thought that the social structure should come alongside such a person to provide him with a basic income to meet his needs. It was and is a very caring idea — one that has a biblical flavor. When God gave commands to Moses about how the people should live, this instruction was given about the Levites:

> This applies to the Levites: Men twenty-five years old or more shall come to take part in the work at the Tent of Meeting, but at the age of fifty, they must retire from their regular service and work no longer. They may assist their brothers in performing their duties at the Tent of Meeting, but they themselves must not do the work.
>
> Numbers 8:24 – 26

This command recognized the natural decline of one's ability to do the work required for the priesthood. Older priests could certainly provide some assistance, but the bulk of the heavy work was reserved for those with the strength and ability.

Although three thousand years ago it may have been absolutely reasonable to count a fifty-year-old in the ranks of "old age," it is quite unreasonable now. Fifty- and sixty-year-olds usually have plenty of strength and ability. Boomers have dramatically changed the way aging happens. Were God to give such a command today, I wonder what the stated age of mandatory retirement would be. It almost certainly would be much older than fifty — perhaps approaching the age of seventy. We have strength and ability long past the Old Testament standard of retirement age.

Time to Keep Working

If truth be told, we don't typically retire because of reduced strength and ability. As people began to live longer and healthier lives during the last half of the twentieth century, we began to think of retirement as leisure. Retirement didn't mean we *couldn't* work any longer; it meant a time when we should reward ourselves with rest, relaxation, and fun for our hard work over many years. Retirement planning didn't focus so much on having enough to survive as on having enough to do all the fun things we always wanted to do or to reach the goals we missed out on when we were younger.

Think about the current stream of retirement commercials on television that aim to convince you that retirement should be the time when you can do just as you always pleased or dreamed. Frankly, I find nothing in Scripture that even remotely resembles this idea of retirement. Our current ideas of retirement — ones we've counted on as our "right" — sound dangerously close to the mind-set of the rich man whom Jesus described as clueless about a meaningful relationship with God:

> And I'll [the rich man] say to myself, "You have plenty of good things laid up for many years. Take life easy; eat, drink and be merry."

But God said to him, "You fool! This very night your life will be demanded from you. Then who will get what you have prepared for yourself?"

Luke 12:19–20

Work is a good thing created by God for our welfare. Work isn't always pleasant, but we are doing a good thing in bringing order out of chaos and providing for our needs. The Bible does teach that the time may come to slow down as our ability and strength fade, but even then we are to keep making a contribution. Perpetual relaxation and desiring a life of no work and all play do not describe a biblical model. As the apostle Paul points out, "We hear that some among you are idle. They are not busy; they are busybodies. Such people we command and urge in the Lord Jesus Christ to settle down and earn the bread they eat. And as for you, brothers, never tire of doing what is right" (2 Thessalonians 3:11–13).

When we think about retirement, we must start with the idea that to work is a good thing. It is good for your creativity and vitality, and it is good to provide for yourself. In a world of shrinking resources, many of us will have to readjust our thinking and refocus our efforts to earn enough to supply our needs. Beyond that, we'll most likely be working to provide for not only our own needs but also for the needs of our aging parents, adult children, and perhaps grandchildren. We may well have the strength and vitality to work until at least age seventy. But even after that age, we must examine the goal of retirement. If our goal is to slow down, conserve strength, work at less strenuous jobs, and take on service that helps younger generations, then I believe we are in sync with the biblical idea. This may include times of visiting family members, enjoying times of recreation, and taking vacations. But if our goal is to simply check out of life and "eat, drink and be merry," then I believe we'll be seeking retirement for a bankrupt reason.

The easiest way, then, to meet our needs is to keep working in our present jobs. Not all of us will have the option to retire. For some of us work will be an absolute necessity if we've been victimized by a lost pension, didn't save enough, or mismanaged our retirement funds. Working is a way to have some income we can count on. Some of us remember the days of salary cap efforts and corporate downsizing in the '80s and '90s, when workers age fifty and older were forced out of their jobs or encouraged to take early retirement. Those days are quickly coming to an end, as the labor market continues to shrink. With fewer workers, employers will be forced to expand the labor pool, and I envision older workers jumping from the bottom of the hiring totem pole to at least an improved position – and maybe even toward the top.

In the next decade, we'll see a distinct shift in the behavior of employers as they try to protect their labor pool by investing more in an effort to hold on to their workers. The liability employers have through the higher salary of older workers is nothing compared to the problems they'll have if there is no one to hire! We'll see more and more employers making changes in their policies to allow workers to continue employment at least until age seventy. It is likely that the government will formulate some type of legislation, because doing so will serve only to enhance the future of retirement programs.

But does this mean you will automatically be more attractive to your employer? Not necessarily. It does mean you'll probably have to refocus and learn new technologies and skills needed by your employer. If you realize that you are likely to be working another ten or fifteen years, or until age seventy, you can shift into the mind-set of learning new skills. Remember that you are a boomer and that you have excelled at adapting and causing change all of your life. If you move yourself from the idea of "slowing down" to the idea of "keeping vital," you'll have little problem in making this adjustment.

Karen was an accountant who had worked for an accounting firm for many years. She had survived all the pressure and layoffs of decades past and held on to make partner in her firm. But as she closed in on age sixty-two, she felt tempted to retire, since she had grandchildren and her mother to care for.

"I thought it would just be easier to move into a caregiving job and enjoy life a little more," she said. "And besides, there was always something new to learn in the accounting field, and it wasn't easy to keep up."

But Karen recognized a real threat to her financial security.

"When I started looking at my mother's finances, I realized that she was surviving almost exclusively on Social Security and that all of her resources were being spent on my father's care. In addition, my daughter had a shaky marriage, and I never knew when she might need my help."

Karen kept on working and revved up her skill level by attending a series of seminars on a new accounting software.

"It was good for me to decide not only to stay but to learn something that no one else in my firm knew. I became a hot item at work, because everyone all of a sudden wanted to know what I knew. I basically rode that wave for another six years, and it made a tremendous difference in my job performance and in my attitude toward the job."

If you need to work to provide for your needs or the needs of others, it is not a good idea merely to hang on a bit longer, but it's much better to energize yourself into making a difference in your work.

These three to five extra years you tack on to your career can make an amazing difference in your financial status during what we think of as retirement years. First, you'll have those additional years of making contributions to a retirement account or some other mechanism that builds your benefits and resources instead of diminishing them. Second, every year you work and do not draw on your retirement resources means one less year of inactivity, which preserves the resource for the years you can't work. Third, if you don't retire until age seventy, it is much more likely that you'll either be at the end of the burden of caring for your aging parents or your aging parent will already have passed. Keeping a job while that burden exists protects you from the financial vulnerability of using your own retirement resources to take care of your parents. Finally, working to an age beyond "normal retirement" often contributes to your mental and physical well-being, which means you will likely live a healthier lifestyle in old age. This in turn reduces your financial vulnerability to sicknesses and hospitalizations.

Can you do it? Can you work until age seventy or perhaps even longer? Of course you can. Most of us have the strength and vitality to work *much* longer than we originally thought possible. But the truth is, with the current state of shrinking resources, it may become a *requirement* to work until age seventy. But even if it never becomes a requirement, many of us will likely have to continue our careers simply to provide for our needs.

Some of us will retire out of our regular jobs because of a mandatory age limit or because the job is too taxing or demanding. In this case, there is still a possibility you will have to work to meet your needs. It is good to identify the job sectors that are seeing the largest growth. Service jobs have a particularly large projected need over the next decade. People are often surprised to find that simple sales jobs or counter jobs can often pay ten to twelve dollars an hour. Manual labor such as ironing or gardening can sometimes yield substantial money. Working part-time in a place where you formerly worked full-time can often be not only appreciated but financially profitable. Former teachers, for instance, who work as substitutes can often make $80 to $100 a day. Skills such as being good with numbers or managing people or offices are usually in high demand and can yield substantial pay for part-time work.

Be creative and challenge yourself to learn new skills. Remember that any income you can generate during normal retirement age means you'll be utilizing less of the resources you have set aside for retirement. In this way, continuing to work is almost always a good strategy to protect yourself and survive the coming flood.

Managing Your Own Health

One issue we tend to overlook is that of managing our health and keeping ourselves as healthy as possible. A ticking time bomb lies hidden in the current array of government services. Medicare is woefully underfunded and is projected to be out of money by 2018. Past efforts to fix Social Security and Medicare have failed miserably, primarily because plans were inadequate or lobby organizations successfully stemmed the tide of cutting benefits.

But Medicare is in significant trouble, and it is doubtful that even if serious efforts began today, they would result in solving the problem. As a result, benefits and coverages will almost certainly be cut—a particularly important reality when we realize that the vast majority of Americans over age sixty-five have their health care coverage through Medicare. It is likely that a larger percentage of the cost of medical care will fall on the boomer generation than on the previous generation, which makes staying healthy much more of a necessity.

The problem is that boomers aren't doing very well in this area of life. Research tells us that people in their mid-fifties report poorer health, more pain, and more trouble doing everyday physical tasks than was true of the previous generation. In addition, the boomer group reports more chronic health conditions and more drinking and psychiatric problems than the older cohort had at a similar time of life. The picture we have of boomers successfully fighting aging every step of the way may be popular in advertising, but the truth is that we have more difficulty walking, climbing steps, getting up from chairs, kneeling, and carrying out normal physical tasks. As a group, we are more out of shape, heavier, and in poorer overall health.

The consequence is that as a group, we are much more likely to need *more* health care than our predecessors, not less. We have grown up in a medical age where we've come to expect that pills and treatments will fix whatever problems we have. But as we age and get various ailments, it will take much more medicine and costly treatments to keep us going. In a time of shrinking resources, one has to wonder if those treatments will continue to be readily available.

We used to think physical decline was just a part of aging so there wasn't much that could be done to keep us vital and strong. We know now, however, that keeping active, exercising, and eating what is good for us makes a tremendous difference. Not only can we maintain our strength and vitality; we can actually get stronger and have more energy. It only makes sense to get on an exercise regimen and lose weight in order to maintain better health. Not only will it make us feel better; it may well reduce our financial vulnerability to rising health costs.

Get Your Financial House in Order

Let me be absolutely clear: the greatest threat to financial well-being during your retirement years is debt. Americans have become convinced that debt is a part of life, as our government now has a national debt that totals almost nine *trillion* dollars. As consumers, we have individual debts that total nearly two and a half trillion dollars. About 45 percent of us spend more than we make, each year going a little further in the hole. Personal bankruptcies have gone up every year over the past two decades and have doubled over the past ten years. The average household carries over $9,000 in credit card debt alone. Americans are in a sea of debt, which causes untold anxiety in individuals, stresses in relationships, and depression and hardship in families. If you carry substantial debt into what you normally think of as your retirement years, you will likely be the one in three boomers who can never retire.

Find Out What Drives You

God declares, "The silver is mine and gold is mine" (Haggai 2:8), but it certainly seems as though we are greatly vested in trying to wrest control of those two commodities away from him. When we have compromised our financial condition, we almost always have a reason that drives us. And if we have any hope of pulling ourselves out of this financial mess, we must first be honest about our motivations.

People who overspend are consumption driven. All of us have grown up in a consumer world in which we are beckoned to spend money everywhere we turn. We see it on television, in advertising, and at movies; we hear it in songs and see it in our peers — and all of it is offered with "no payments for a year."

But this is only part of the story. Many of us are driven to spend because it makes us feel powerful. We reason that somehow we deserve to have the best, and so we feel shortchanged if we don't have what others have. Perhaps our drive comes from the embarrassment we felt as a child when we didn't have something as nice as someone else or when someone made fun of the things we had or the way we dressed. Perhaps it comes from the desire to show people that we can take charge and impress others. Perhaps it just comes from feeling the need to keep up with those who have much. Whatever the case, as we overspend from the "power" angle, we are driven by our desire to achieve some type of status.

The problem with status, of course, is that there is no real end to the things you "need" – because all your possessions never really fill the void. It is a little like trying to fill up on cotton candy, which has substance but quickly disappears. If you are driven by status, you know the feeling of having to have that new car, new house, or new clothes, only to move on to wanting something "new" almost immediately. When we use things to build our self-esteem or to make ourselves feel OK, we are on an endless path of purchasing, because our things never make us anything different. Our identity and power can come only from God. And make no mistake, God makes sure that when we try to find our identity in things, we are doomed to failure.

Listen to what God said to the Israelites when they returned from captivity and spent their time adorning their paneled houses instead of rebuilding the temple: "Give careful thought to your ways. You have planted much, but have harvested little. You eat, but never have enough. You drink, but never have your fill. You put on clothes, but are not warm. You earn wages, only to put them in a purse with holes in it" (Haggai 1:5–6). If you are driven to spend money by a desire for power and status, you should also give careful thought to your ways. Do not seek that which cannot satisfy, but ground your identity in God.

Sometimes we feel driven to spend money because we feel anxious or depressed and want to feel better. Essentially, we spend money because we believe it will help us escape. Maybe in our depression we need some cheering up – nothing that a trip to the mall and some new clothes or shoes won't solve! Or perhaps we're under too much stress at work – we can always spend money for a recreational trip out of town or a new gadget for our car, computer, or house. Or maybe we're just plain bored and think the answer is to spend money on something. And in what seems to be the ultimate in the "tiger eating its own tail," we often feel under the gun because of financial stress, so we go on a trip or spending spree to make us feel better.

If this kind of behavior sounds at all familiar, know you are in good company. Well over 60 percent of people who have excessive debt spend money to try to make themselves feel better. While it is understandable to want to use money as a source of enjoyment, to use it to escape our bad feelings only complicates our depression and anxiety.

Spending cannot make us feel better any more than it can give us a sense of identity. Only God—only resting in him—can ultimately give us relief from anxiety and depression. As Peter urges, "Humble yourselves, therefore, under God's mighty hand, that he may lift you up in due time. Cast all your anxiety on him because he cares for you" (1 Peter 5:6–7).

Make a Plan and a Budget

I hope you realize that if you are being driven by a desire for power or by anxiety, you must first address these issues with God. You must find out what drives you, and then you will be more realistic and more capable of utilizing the benefits that a budget and a plan can offer you.

Budgeting can be as easy or as complicated as you want it to be. Basically, a budget takes what you make and balances it with what you spend. Some people feel comfortable detailing specific categories for each area of household expenses and keeping meticulous records on the amount to spend in each area. Others feel most comfortable taking a specific overall figure of income and just making sure that the checkbook does not exceed that amount. Whether or not you are detailed, the heart of the budget is to ensure that you do not spend more than what you make – and that you stick to the discipline of not incurring more debt!

I am a fan of the budget that spends, saves, and gives. Any budget from a Christian perspective must, I believe, have a component of giving. Although people differ on whether a specific percentage is required of Christians, all would agree that Christians should give of their resources. The primary reason, of course, is that we give in recognition that everything belongs to God. But giving also challenges our natural inclination to depend on ourselves. When we give, especially when we are in debt and do not have what we think is enough, it forces us into a position of depending on God. The prophet Malachi reveals God's desire: "Bring the whole tithe into the storehouse, that there may be food in my house. Test me in this," says the LORD Almighty, "and see if I will not throw open the floodgates of heaven and pour out so much blessing that you will not have room enough for it" (Malachi 3:10). I don't believe this verse guarantees riches if we give, but I do think it guarantees enough – even an abundance – if we give.

I also believe it is essential to save, which is difficult when you are buried under a load of debt. The first savings plan to incorporate into your goal of making a budget work is to get an emergency fund in place that can keep you from running up debt when you hit unpredictable expenses. The secret of an emergency fund is actually funding it every month. Such a fund starts off small, but if you fund it every month, it can grow into a substantial insulation against incurring additional debt in the case of unexpected expenses. Of course, it takes discipline to not spend the emergency fund on useless things or on things we justify as necessities.

Budgets have a positive impact on the debt problem only if

you are willing to "bite the bullet" and reduce your current living expenses. Think in terms of living on the bare minimum for a period of time, such as a year or two. Try to save money on everything possible, from the food you eat to the way you dress. And avoid spending money on big-ticket items! Drive that car until the wheels fall off, and try to fix everything or do without where possible. Keep spending at an absolute minimum. Whatever you do, resist the temptation to use a loan or credit card to pay for something. Even small charges on a credit card add up and can throw off a budget. If you use a budget correctly, you should see money begin to be freed up to pay down debts.

There is some wisdom in restructuring debt to gain lower interest rates. It is also wise to investigate whether your credit card companies and banks are willing to negotiate lower interest rates or realistic payment options. But spend the bulk of your time and effort in actually producing money to eliminate debt. The best plans I've seen start with the smallest debt and pay it off completely. This may mean you make minimum payments on other debts while you eliminate the smallest, but the goal is to begin getting the debts paid off, one by one. You'll find great encouragement as you begin to see how progress can be made by permanently getting creditors out of your hair! Target creditors one by one until you eliminate each one.

Two notes of caution: First, be wary of "nonprofit" debt resolution services or debt reduction plan services. A significant number of these companies are exclusively in the business of debt restructuring for their own profit or for the good of the companies they represent. You'll often be much better served by speaking directly to the credit card company or bank to negotiate more favorable payments or interest rates. Second, be wary of home equity loans that consolidate debt. While this strategy can be useful to get you back on your feet financially, if you are unable to meet your payment obligations, you run the risk of losing your home to the organization that made the loan. There is simply no easy way out of debt, and promised quick fixes or easy solutions are most likely deceptive.

Remember that in most instances you have the ability to produce additional resources. I've seen people make significant progress in debt reduction by selling some of their things they don't use or need any longer. It may also be helpful to work part-time for a period to target debt elimination. It is very difficult to put in fifty to sixty-five hours of work a week, but the benefit of pulling oneself out of debt is often worth the sacrifice. Be aware, though, that the more you work, the more you tend to think you "deserve" a break or a treat. People who work additional hours often fall into the trap of spending more money on eating out or on entertaininment.

How far should your debt elimination go? As far as you can make it go before you hit retirement—and the further the better. Certainly you should eliminate all short-term loans and credit card debt. I also believe you should eliminate all car loans and student loans. This same strategy that eliminates small debts can also work with large debts. Many adopt a plan to pay off one's mortgage. For a person in financial trouble, to do so may seem to be a stretch, but it isn't as far-fetched as it seems. For one thing, boomers typically have owned their house for many years, so the actual balance on a thirty-year loan may not be quite so daunting anymore. What's more, it's amazing to see how disciplined you've become as you've been working on elim-inating debt and how that same discipline can be applied to pay-ing off a mortgage. The apostle Paul urges that debt elimination be a priority for all believers: "Let no debt remain outstanding, except the continuing debt to love one another, for he who loves his fellowman has fulfilled the law" (Romans 13:8).

If you can eliminate debt, you will have taken a big step in setting yourself up for surviving the eventual flood at retirement. Not only will you protect yourself from paying out money you don't have; you'll be able to begin putting significant amounts of money into savings. If you are fifty-five right now, you'll likely work until age sixty-eight or seventy. If you can eliminate your debt within five years – not only possible but reasonable – then you'll have ten years to build additional resources for your aging years. Even if you were able to save only an additional $100 a month, at a modest growth rate you could accumulate over $20,000. This may not sound like much, but it actually translates into a resource that can provide you and your family with over a year of living expenses if it is allowed to grow until the end of your retirement. Eliminating debt gets the financial ball rolling in the direction of accumulating instead of spending.

What's Your Retirement Personality?

Take a good look at yourself and evaluate your personality. How we handle the adversity on the horizon for all of us – and imminent disaster for a fair number of us – will depend to a large extent on our personalities.

How do we identify our retirement personality? It will probably be the personality you now have. The way you handle difficulties, stress, and challenges now is likely a precursor to the way you will handle those challenges in fifteen to twenty-five years.

People often ask me if I believe that people's personalities change with age. Although I recognize that some changes happen because of dementia or brain damage, I typically respond, "No, people become more of who they always were." Having said that, I think it's helpful to think about how boomers will adjust to the retirement problems ahead.

PERSONALITY TYPE 1: Troopers

One group of folks are process oriented, willing to do whatever is necessary to solve problems, loyal to the task, and faithful to get work completed. I call these types of people *troopers*.

These individuals don't spend much time asking why something happened; they focus more on what has to be done to correct the situation or make things turn out OK. Troopers are usually hard-working folks who don't complain and don't ask many questions. They bless people through their patient and faithful service.

Troopers will do great with the challenges that retirement will present because they have generally done well with similar challenges in life. Generally, I find that these troopers have done adequate, good financial planning for their later years, but the reality is that it won't matter much; somehow troopers will find a way to meet needs, no matter what challenges lie ahead.

One weakness of troopers, however, is that they complain so little that they often neglect some of their own needs, which can put their health in jeopardy. Troopers keep going, no matter how they feel, and this can have detrimental results when they fail to take care of themselves properly.

PERSONALITY TYPE 2: Edgers

Edgers are the "in between" of every personality type. They tend to be very resilient when it comes to adapting to new things but usually feel somewhat anxious in anticipating the change. They tend to keep several options open, not committing to any one course of action wholeheartedly. As a result, they tend to work—but often at less intense jobs or on a part-time basis. They tend to travel and relax some but carefully schedule downtimes around others' schedules or work demands. They are willing to cut back but don't usually make the kind of wholesale sacrifices typical of troopers.

Are they good workers, adjusters, grandparents, caregivers, lovers of life? The answers are, "Yes." "Yes." "Yes." And "Yes, most of the time." The anxiousness of the edgers tends to drive out a good part of their vitality and energy. If you are around edgers enough, you usually get the feeling they are just about ready to be happy or sure of themselves, but they don't quite ever go all the way.

Edgers will make it because they are at least aware of the problems on the horizon, and when challenges come, they typically respond in a positive and responsible manner.

PERSONALITY TYPE 3: Seekers

Seekers are an adventuresome lot who tend to look for new opportunities and the freedom to express themselves and take on new experiences. I have seen seekers who move toward retirement without fear and with a willingness to try anything—from investing all they have in new businesses such as a restaurant to taking unusual risks such as learning to skydive at age seventy.

We tend to love seekers because at least a part of us wishes we were more like them—fearless, adventuresome, and carefree. But they definitely have a downside. They tend to be so "in the moment" that they forget they must last for the long haul. Their "devil may care" attitude may work for experiencing great adventures but may play havoc with the reality of dealing with health limitations and providing for themselves over the thirty to thirty-five years they'll be living in retirement. Some seekers burn through their resources within ten to fifteen years, and some lose their resources altogether through risky investments or failed businesses. Seekers are great fun, but it definitely is no fun if you have to pick up the pieces for them after their health fails and they've run out of money.

PERSONALITY TYPE 4: Withdrawers

Withdrawers tend to retreat from the world and "shrink" their worlds smaller and smaller as they get older and do things in set patterns. Withdrawers don't like to get involved, so they have very few close relationships and tend to be somewhat reclusive. It's not that they don't take care of their own business, because most withdrawers are very responsible at getting their tasks accomplished and resolved. In terms of managing their homes, bills, and immediate families, they are usually quite competent and satisfied.

Withdrawers, however, are not as competent in areas requiring adjustment. Resourcefulness isn't their forte; they tend to resist change and make situations worse when forced to change. They would much rather take care of themselves and let the world take care of itself.

The problem, of course, is that in the next few decades of retirement, there will be a potential for *many* changes in which retirees are likely to have to make more and more adjustments as they age, not fewer.

We All Need to Change

No matter what type of retirement personality we have, the next thirty years will provide plenty of areas in which we'll need to change. It is simply inefficient and ineffective to proclaim, "I am who I am, and I'm too old to change," or "I've lived long enough to behave the way I want to behave." Your personality is not static; it is meant to grow.

We boomers will live longer than any generation before us—and probably a good five years longer than our parents. Our lives, no matter how old we are, are meant to change and meet the challenges God brings our way.

Troopers will need to be more in tune with taking care of themselves, while edgers will need to deal with their own anxieties. Seekers will have to be more responsible and grounded in reality, while withdrawers will have to be more adaptable and open to new living situations.

The apostle Paul declares, "Now the Lord is the Spirit, and where the Spirit of the Lord is, there is freedom. And we, who with unveiled faces all reflect the Lord's glory, are being transformed into his likeness with ever-increasing glory, which comes from the Lord, who is the Spirit" (2 Corinthians 3:17 – 18). There is no time limit on this transformation into the likeness of Christ. Make up your mind *now* to meet the challenges of your retirement with growth and openness to change.

8

MAKING THE FINANCES WORK

My mother was a child of the Great Depression, so she knows how to scrimp and save and stretch every last use out of an object before it is totally used up. She buys many of her clothes at secondhand shops and then puts miles on those clothes that the original owner never thought possible. I have seldom seen her throw out food, and I'm always surprised when I have a tasty cake or snack at her house that I later find out has been stowed away in the freezer for months. Old ketchup bottles get precariously balanced upside down so every last drop can be salvaged before discarding the bottle.

Boomers aren't nearly as accustomed to making sure things are used up, but we will have to learn the trick of the ketchup bottle with our retirement resources. We will live longer than any previous generation, yet most of us will have the option to retire at a relatively young age. And so we may have thirty to thirty-five years to make our retirement finances work. As anyone who has been retired awhile can tell you, it is not the front end of retirement that is the financial challenge, but making the resources last until the tail end of life. The first decade – between ages sixty-five and seventy-five – won't present the real challenge, but the way we utilize our resources during that first decade *will* go a long way in determining whether we will have enough resources throughout the second decade and into our third decade of retirement.

I said earlier that it is a very good idea to deal with this problem, at least initially, by continuing to work. About one-third of us are a retirement disaster waiting to happen – those of us who have worked for companies that have defaulted on pensions and those of us who have lost a substantial amount of our resources to fraud, as well as a good number of us who thought we were responsibly augmenting our retirement savings, only to find that we either didn't invest enough or invested the funds in instruments that didn't produce adequate return. If you are part of this one-third, then you will have no choice but to continue to work to take care of your obligations.

But even if you aren't a part of this one-third, I still believe it is good to work until you are at least age seventy – and perhaps as old as seventy-five. Some of us will be "old" at seventy, and certainly at age seventy-five, but I anticipate that as many as 80 percent of us will still be performing the bulk of middle-age activities quite competently at age seventy-five. If you are able to avoid using your retirement resources before age seventy or even seventy-five – and indeed, if you continue to build those resources – there is a good chance that when you choose to stop working, you can use the bulk of your time to contribute in any way you wish. If, however, you do choose to retire at age sixty-five, sixty-six, or sixty-seven, you will need to plan wisely and give careful thought as to how you will live.

Utilizing Your Resources

Begin by getting an idea of how you will utilize the resources you have. Each person is different, and it's hard to know if these resources will be stable or predictable, but it is still necessary to plan and to be as prudent as possible. Generally, people will have a combination of the following resources available at retirement: Social Security; Medicare or other medical insurance; pensions; individual retirement accounts (IRAs) and annuities; and retirement accounts associated with work.

RESOURCE 1: Social Security

Social Security provides the majority of income for most older Americans, and for about one-third of them, it will be the sole source of their income. There are all sorts of caveats to Social Security, given current government projections that the program can be funded only at a two-thirds level by 2040. Significant efforts may be undertaken to "save" this program, since it is the lion's share of income for so many people, but it is far too soon to tell. Right now, the best we can do is describe what is currently true and provide hints of what to expect in the future.

Although most people have no choice about whether to participate in Social Security, there are major exceptions. If you work for the federal government or if you've retired from the military, you are covered by a different program and trust fund. In addition, you may not have been required to participate in Social Security if you worked for a company with a pension program (for example, the railroad, airlines, or an educational organization). But note that even if you didn't contribute to Social Security through these sources, you may have had employment through another source in which you did contribute. Normally, you will have needed forty quarters of work in which you paid into Social Security to qualify for some type of benefits. This is ten years' worth of work, and it doesn't have to be ten continuous quarters. Many people, even late in life, can put in the necessary quarters to receive Social Security benefits at a later age.

You may also qualify to receive Social Security if your spouse qualifies or your deceased spouse qualified, or in some cases, if your ex-spouse qualifies. The number of quarters you've earned over the qualifying amount has no effect on your benefit amount. Average earnings over your work career will determine your annual benefit from Social Security.

You can begin receiving your Social Security benefits as early as age sixty-two, but doing so will greatly reduce the amount of benefit you are entitled to receive. Depending on when you were born, your monthly retirement amount will be reduced by 25 to 30 percent. Boomers born between 1946 and 1954 can reach full retirement age at sixty-six. For those born between 1955 and 1959, the age creeps up by two months for each year you were born past 1954, and for those born after 1960, the full retirement age is sixty-seven. It is also important to note that you can increase your benefits from Social Security if you delay retirement past your full retirement age. Generally, your yearly benefit increases 8 percent for every year you delay retirement, up to age seventy. Currently, after age seventy, the benefit increase no longer applies if you delay taking Social Security.

It is also important to realize that you can be employed and receive Social Security benefits. If you are under full retirement age, the limit for earnings is currently $12,960. This includes only earnings from work – not from pensions or other retirement income sources. For every two dollars you earn over this limit, your benefit will be reduced by one dollar. Once you reach your full retirement age, you can receive your full Social Security benefits with no deductions, no matter how much income you earn. Earnings may, however, be reduced from other pensions or annuities that you receive.

If you currently qualify for Social Security, you may be receiving a regular statement estimating what your monthly benefit will be and the benefit your spouse will receive. Note that if your spouse also qualifies for Social Security, he or she will receive the benefit owed under their own work instead of a spousal benefit, unless the spousal benefit is higher. Several months before you actually retire, you should apply for your benefits. To do this you will need your Social Security number, your birth certificate, proof of citizenship or lawful status, military discharge papers, and your W–2 form or tax return form from the previous year.

When should you apply? I believe it is best not to retire early with Social Security. It's not a matter of whether you'll end up not getting the same benefit amount—you will because you'll be drawing the benefit longer; it's a matter of maximizing your resources throughout the long retirement years. Regardless of the fact that you'll receive the same benefit amount over a lifetime, if you begin receiving benefits early, your income from Social Security in any one year will be 30 percent less. Toward the end of your life, with your other resources depleted, this 30 percent in any one year could spell the difference between being able to afford rent, food, and medication and not being able to afford them. So work in order to *increase* your eventual Social Security benefit.

I say this also because I anticipate that at some point, there will be either a benefit reduction or a freeze put on Social Security increases. I believe that boomers will receive some benefit from Social Security, but the amount is likely to be reduced by one-third, compared to what our parents received, in terms of inflation-adjusted dollars. If you begin taking benefits early, the amount is further reduced by freezes or cuts. You could eventually be trying to survive on only one-third of the benefit that your parents had available to them. Besides, Social Security itself estimates that your maximum benefit is likely to replace only 40 percent of what you earned in your working days. Work as long as you can and delay these benefits, so that when you do receive them, they will be the maximum amount possible.

RESOURCE 2: Medicare or Other Medical Insurances

No one has to remind us that health care costs have risen in the last twenty years, and so it is no surprise that those costs are projected to rise similarly in the coming decades. Along with these costs, the cost of medical insurance has risen dramatically. There is simply no way to predict how this issue will eventually be resolved. It was only about twenty years ago that a physician and patient had almost total control over personal health decisions, which were almost always based on the idea of getting the "best care available" for the patient. But with the advent of managed care and the effort to control cost, these decisions now include the insurance company as well. Instead of the "best care" concept, the framework has shifted to "reasonable care" and includes the ideas of cost, likely diagnosis, and most efficient treatment.

It is almost totally accepted in the health care industry today that cost issues will be a driving force in determining care for the patient. It has been a subtle but dynamic shift in the way consumers expect to have their health needs taken care of by the medical community. But even with this shift, there has been no decrease in the cost of health care, and expenses continue to skyrocket. The reality is that even though health insurance is very expensive, it is much too risky to be without it. Those with no coverage risk subpar indigent care or expenses that can lead to financial ruin in a matter of days.

Many companies and organizations have private or contract health plans in which they allow their retired employees to participate at regular employee rates. If you did not pay Medicare taxes when you were employed, these plans are by far the most inexpensive to maintain while you are retired. However, there is risk, as companies and organizations regularly switch plans and change rules. There are always issues and potential risks with former employers staying solvent or remaining in business. If a company goes under, the benefits that go with that company are likely to disappear or be drastically changed.

Most people will prefer to be covered by Medicare – the government program for health insurance. You can qualify for Medicare at age sixty-five, even if you continue working past that age. Medicare has four major parts (see also "Paying for Medical Assistance," pages 88 – 90):

- *Part A* generally covers costs associated with hospitalizations. If you paid Medicare taxes throughout your employment, you pay nothing for Medicare Part A. If you didn't pay these taxes, the cost can be significant (over $400 a month currently). Please note, however, that Part A covers only part of the cost associated with hospitalization; the patient is usually responsible for 20 percent of the total costs, plus any deductibles that apply.

- *Part B* covers costs associated with doctor visits and care. The cost for this insurance depends on your annual income but currently runs from a monthly premium of $90 to greater than $160. This coverage is optional, and there are additional costs and deductibles with services provided.

- *Part C* is an option to participating in Part A and Part B that basically combines benefits in those two programs into a managed care option in regions where these plans are available. While costs are a bit higher than Parts A and B, premiums vary according to the managed care organization chosen and the contract services provided. Like any health care managed by this type of organization, participants agree to seek services from selected physicians and organizations.

- *Part D* is the prescription drug benefit managed under a variety of plans. Generally, if a person chooses a managed care option under Part C, they will have some type of prescription drug coverage. If a person is in Part A and B, then they will usually select a plan under Part D that covers most of the prescription drugs they need. Premiums for Part D are determined by service area.

Medicare is a reasonable and reliable health care insurance program, but significant costs attach to each part of the plan. In order to manage these costs, many retired persons opt for "medigap" insurance contracted for by private companies and generally designed to provide payment for deductibles and percentages not covered by Medicare. These companies, however, are not part of the Medicare program, so consumers must be careful. Medicare holds a list of generally reputable medigap insurance providers. You should look carefully at the coverage that each provides and make sure it gives the security you seek at a reasonable cost.

What will happen to Medicare? Certainly it cannot continue to exist without some major changes. Current government projections predict that the program will be bankrupt within ten to twelve years. It seems inconceivable that the government would let this program dissolve and let so many retirees fend for themselves, but then again, the government currently lets millions of children and infants go uninsured or underinsured. Perhaps the Medicare crisis will eventually lead to the development of some type of national health care insurance. But even if the government chooses to "solve" the health care crisis in this way, severe funding problems will continue because of the decreasing number of workers in the labor pool over the next decades. Boomers headed toward retirement can expect that health care and health insurance will be more expensive, that insurance will provide less coverage, and that retirees will pick up more of the cost.

One way to protect yourself from such financial unknowns is to seek long-term care insurance. Private insurance companies write these policies and offer a variety of options for full-time institutional care, from full payment to partial payment to providing a set sum for home care. These policies are generally expensive but can provide a net of security if ill health or Alzheimer's runs in the family. The premiums become more expensive as a person ages, so the sooner a person starts paying for coverage, the less the premiums are likely to be.

RESOURCE 3: Pensions

Although increasingly fewer organizations offer pensions as a part of a benefit package, many boomers have participated at one time or another. In traditional pension plans, either you or your employer, or both, set aside money for you. Then the employer or a contract organization managed the money and "guaranteed" a specific amount of monthly income after you retired. How much you received depended on the length of your employment and the amount of your earnings. The advantage of a traditional pension program was that they paid a monthly check and the benefit continued for as long as you lived. Most of these pension programs had a "vesting" period – a stated number of years of participation in the program in order to get the full benefit. Spouses usually continued to receive the pension check even after the former employee died.

A more common pension plan today is called a "cash balance

plan." In such programs, the employer makes a contribution to an employee account. Even though the employer may manage the account, all principal and interest amounts in the employee account stay in the employee account. The employer manages all the risks and rewards, and when the employee retires, he or she receives either a lump sum payment or payments that are spread out. The advantage of these types of pensions is that the employee clearly knows what is in his or her account and can track it carefully. The accounts are not subject to other variables such as company health or number of employees participating in the pension. But the pension performance or amount of pay-off is not guaranteed.

Pensions, of course, have suffered greatly over the last several decades, and adequate return is in question for many retirees who for years devoted themselves to their companies. If you are in a pension program, you should consult with the company's human resources personnel to determine the health of the pension program, the projected problems, and the rates of return. If the pension is in trouble, don't just hope for the best, but try to invest every resource you can afford into some type of annuity or individual retirement account. If your pension program goes belly-up, at least part of the money is insured by a government program; but you will probably have to augment your income needs by working for a much longer period of time.

RESOURCE 4: Individual Retirement Accounts and Annuities

Individual retirement accounts (IRAs) and annuities offer two benefits: (1) they provide a way to tax-defer or shelter income, and (2) they can provide significant resources for retirement. Although a variety of IRAs are available to employees and self-employed individuals, most of them allow an amount of money to be set aside, up to a maximum set by the government, that can be tax deferred – a big advantage because individual tax rates are usually much lower as incomes are typically smaller in our older years. IRAs are usually managed by insurance companies or money managers in mutual fund instruments.

Annuities can be complicated, but essentially they offer a way for an individual to tax-shelter money that will in turn be used for income in retirement. You can purchase an annuity through either a premium payment each month or a lump sum contract. Annuities are a contract between you and an insurance company, and the insurance company takes responsibility for the investing and managing of the money. In return, you receive either a guaranteed lump sum payment on retirement or a monthly income for life.

With both IRAs and annuities, it is essential that you make sure the company or product you are purchasing is reliable. Many unscrupulous or incompetent managers have used these instruments to mislead and sometimes defraud individuals of their hard-earned funds. Also, not all IRAs and annuities give the same rate of return. Do careful research to determine whether the rates of return are comparable to stock market or bond programs. Also, be wary of costs and hidden fees. If an IRA is underperforming in relation to the market, it is possible and advisable to roll over the IRA into another instrument. Rolling over is a common practice and you shouldn't hesitate to do it if you are not getting a fair return or are being charged unreasonable fees. Simply stated, you need to pay close attention to the growth pattern of these investments.

RESOURCE 5: Retirement Accounts Associated with Work

An employer's answer to traditional pensions is 401(k) plans in private companies, 457 plans in public and nonprofit sectors, and 403(b) plans in education and nonprofit companies.

In these plans, you and your employer usually contribute to an individual retirement account in your name that you manage. The money you contribute is usually tax deferred and allows you the advantage of taking the money in retirement when your tax rate is likely to be less. While there is a maximum yearly contribution, those who are age fifty and older are encouraged to put in extra money to catch up on retirement investment. Employers usually match whatever the employee puts into the account, up to a set maximum.

These types of accounts have some sound advantages. The employer contributes additional money, the employee is free to choose the IRA, and he or she is responsible for account management. But they have some disadvantages as well. Companies often choose these types of retirement instruments as a way to escape the behemoth costs of traditional pension programs, so it actually costs employers much less and requires more of an investment from the employee. In addition, boomer employees may not be savvy about investment choices or understand what is or is not a good rate of return.

No matter what kind of investment you are accumulating—IRAs, annuities, 401(k) or similar accounts, stocks, bonds, mutual funds, or precious metals—you must keep in mind that you are the captain of your own ship. Companies that have defaulted on their pension obligations found out how difficult it is to effectively manage resources for decades and make good on promised returns. In response to many dismal performances, companies have turned the job of investing over to you to see how effectively you will be able to do the job.

It isn't easy, by any means. Conventional wisdom says you'll need to make about 7 percent annually on investments to be able to secure your retirement goals. Of course, in some years you will do much better than 7 percent; but your portfolio must also weather the down years. In the end, whether you've made good choices or poor ones, you must wisely utilize the investment funds you have. If you are to make the money last over twenty to thirty years of retirement, you must be realistic about what you can afford to withdraw each year. No matter how much or how little you've invested, it is probably prudent to withdraw only 3 to 5 percent of the initial investment per year in order to have enough to last throughout retirement. Remember, it is important to meet your needs not only at the beginning of the retirement years but at the end as well.

And don't forget, you may live as much as 25 to 30 percent of your life as a retired person—or at least at a retirement age. It makes sense to be aggressive with investments in your younger years and get more conservative as retirement nears. But you must also continue to maintain a reasonable growth rate for your investments while you are retired. Never slip into complacency, assuming that investment instruments that have worked well in the past will continue to work well in the future. Even when retired, you should look for investments to gain the 7 percent growth rate. This will necessitate maintaining at least a conservative to moderately aggressive investment stance throughout your lifetime. While the rate of inflation has remained relatively stable in the United States for a long time, even a low rate of inflation requires that our investments keep growing in order to keep pace.

Making Wise Choices

Work as long as you can, invest wisely, and then carefully plan how to utilize the resources you have. Doing these things will help you make sure you gather as many resources as possible for your retirement years. But you can also do some things to monitor your spending and make wise choices to help ensure that your resources last for your entire retirement.

Look at Where You Live

Boomers seem fascinated by their houses. We have generally followed our parents' lead in trying to get "as much house" as we can afford. But there comes a time when doing so doesn't make sense.

It used to be that you had to wait until you were fifty-five to get a once-in-a-lifetime tax break for selling your primary dwelling. Married boomers can now take advantage of earning up to $500,000 on the sale of their house without having to pay income taxes on the gain. If you can free up money in terms of a smaller house payment and use at least part of the money for income during retirement, it may make sense for you to sell a home. Boomers often will do better in a smaller place that doesn't require as much maintenance.

Another good option is to form a multigenerational household. You can move in one of two directions: (1) If you are a boomer caring for an aging parent, you may want to move into the house with your parent. Often these houses are already paid for, and you can use the money you get from the sale of your home to prepare for your own retirement. (2) You may want to move in with your children or have your children move in with you. The twenty-first century will place enormous stresses on the family. Having additional adults in the home may offer more support and provide a better environment in which to raise children.

Many families intentionally move in with grandparents in order for the grandparents to provide child care support and nurture. Dual-income families also like the idea of gaining a larger "labor resource" to manage the house. Besides driving down housing costs for parents and adult children, such an arrangement can provide a positive atmosphere — as long as the generations can cooperate and get along well.

For boomers, such strategies offer a boon for freeing up additional resources for retirement years. It can also give boomers a great connection with their children and grandchildren and provide a sense of belonging and being truly needed.

If you are tempted to think you couldn't live with your parent or your children, consider recent census figures. Multigenerational households have increased in the United States for the past thirty years and may make up as many as 23 percent of all households. Even if you have your house entirely paid for, sharing a home can save dramatically on taxes and insurance. This growing trend may provide a way to maximize your family resources.

Watch Out for Spending

American boomers spend too much. We are likely to spend *way* too much when we reach our retirement years. Once we slow down at our work or stop working altogether, we will likely have more time to shop and participate in costly activities. We also may tend to see ourselves as having more resources to spend on ourselves and others—at least at the beginning of our retirement years. If we are to make these resources last for the long haul, we have to resist the temptation to spend money without giving it much careful thought.

A major way to cut expenses during retirement years is to make sure you don't purchase items on credit. As your retirement goes on, the amount of income you have will become more and more "fixed." If you use this fixed income to pay for interest charges, you will be paying much more for goods and services—and you won't be able to make it up as you did when you were bringing in a work income. Instead, try to save cash until you have enough to make purchases, such as for furniture, clothes, appliances, and even cars. This way of thinking is different from the normal boomer mentality that advocates buying on credit, but you'll find that your dollars will go much further. If you pay cash, you'll probably have to plan your purchases much more wisely and resist impulse buying.

Speaking of cash, it's best to carry as little as possible. While paying cash for items is a good way to counter debt, it's very easy to use it to buy on impulse and to lose track of how much you spend. So pay cash—but carry only the cash you need to make specific and planned purchases. If you must carry a card, carry a debit card that subtracts directly from your account. Be sure to clarify, however, that it is *only* a debit card, as many banks now have cards that will count the balance in a credit card account if there is insufficient money in your account.

Don't be afraid to adopt a "downsizing" mentality. Downsizing doesn't refer only to housing. You may want to downsize with regard to the vehicle you drive—perhaps purchasing a small, fuel-efficient car, or perhaps sharing a car with a spouse or friend. It amazes me how many people have vehicles they use only two or three times a week. Also if your health permits, don't forget to think about bicycling not only as a mode of exercise but as a primary mode of transportation. You can also consider the same principle of downsizing in terms of many common household "necessities." Sharing a lawnmower or a storage unit is a simple way to cut costs without noticing any difference in service.

Remember to look for the small things that can be cut. Look for the best deals and the lowest fees, from insurance companies to financial institutions. Don't be afraid to ask your doctor to write prescriptions for generic drugs. Lower the thermostat, eat out less, and be careful about wasting food. Use coupons. Just keep squeezing pennies out of those dollars, and you'll make progress toward stretching your resources to last the entire length of your retirement.

Trusting in the Boomer Way

I often liken boomers to characters in the Bible. Of everyone I've read about in Scripture, I most often think of the patriarch Joseph.

Joseph was a favored child who knew from the beginning that he was special. His father recognized him as special, treated him as his favorite, and gave him a beautiful coat. When his brothers got upset about this preferential treatment, Joseph made no apologies but instead unwisely told them about a dream in which he predicted they would one day serve him. Confident, rash, and lavished with love—that was Joseph, and it reminds me of how we boomers reveled in our advantaged positions and felt confident in our answers for all of society's problems.

But there's more to the biblical description of Joseph. Yes, he was a dreamer, but he also had to deal with the harsh realities of treachery, enslavement, exploitation, and alienation. Yet in all of Joseph's troubles, we never find him giving up or giving in; we simply find him doing the next right thing and adjusting to whatever happened to him.

He spent the greater part of his life making major adjustments until finally, because of a severe famine, he saw the purpose behind God's plan. With God's favor he won a powerful government position, second only to Pharaoh. Joseph designed and executed a plan to make it through the terrible drought. When his long-lost brothers appeared on the scene to obtain food, all the pain and turmoil of his life suddenly made sense. And so he gave this message to his frightened siblings:

> "Do not be distressed and do not be angry with yourselves for selling me here, because it was to save lives that God sent me ahead of you. For two years now there has been famine in the land, and for the next five years there will not be plowing and reaping. But God sent me ahead

of you to preserve for you a remnant on earth and to save your lives by a great deliverance. So then, it was not you who sent me here, but God."

Genesis 45:5–8

In many respects, we boomers are like the adaptable Joseph. Our retirement years are likely to see more of us in the aging class than ever before, competing for fewer resources than existed for the previous generation. It would be easy to adopt an attitude of dread, apprehension, or anxiety. For all the criticism we boomers have endured for being irresponsible and selfish, we have proven to be highly resilient, forward-looking, and adaptable. We have a history of making change work, just as Joseph did.

We cannot predict what will happen with regard to financial pressures in the coming years. Frankly, the next three decades seem to present problems too big to fix. But if the Lord doesn't return, more than ample evidence suggests that boomers will not only survive this difficult time but thrive in it. We will see what happens throughout these tumultuous retirement decades and no doubt suffer through some injustices, exploitations, and alienations. But I am confident we will respond, adapt, and show the younger generations how to change in order to meet these challenges. We need to trust God but also ourselves and the abilities he has given us.

I don't pretend to know why we have been chosen for this time and place, but I do believe that in the coming decades we will see, just as Joseph saw, why it was necessary for us to go through this intense time of shrinking resources. More than that, I believe we will see how God has used us to change the course of history.

9

BOOMERS GOING OUT WITH A BANG

Hebrews 11 features what is known in evangelical circles as the "Faith Hall of Fame." It highlights remarkable heroes of the faith who believed God for who he is, what he has said, and what he promises to do. "By faith" appears over and over again, as the chapter recounts the legendary actions of Noah, Abraham, Jacob, Joseph, Moses, Gideon, and David.

But alongside the names of the "greats" appear some of the "smalls" – who had just as much faith. Abel, Enoch, and even the humble prostitute Rahab are remembered for their trust in God and their faithful obedience. We also find an extensive listing of the great "unknowns" of the faith, unnamed believers who were equally faithful and true to the word and work of God:

> Others were tortured and refused to be released, so that they might gain a better resurrection. Some faced jeers and flogging, while still others were chained and put in prison.

They were stoned; they were sawed in two; they were put to death by the sword. They went about in sheepskins and goatskins, destitute, persecuted and mistreated – the world was not worthy of them.

Hebrews 11:35 – 38

The boomer generation stands on the precipice of a sea change in the way American life and family are done. More and more we have been forced out onto the ledge by the pressing needs of caregiving for our parents, the discouragement and challenges of our adult children and even their children, and the difficulties of our own aging and the problems of financing our long lives. We're very likely not going to be stoned or flogged, chained or imprisoned, or even forced to wear goatskins. But make no mistake about the next three decades – we *will* be challenged to live by faith.

We will find ourselves swimming in an ocean of need, with problems that seem to defy solution. We will have fewer and fewer resources to call on as we struggle to meet this need. And we will feel exhausted as every day we will be called on to rise up and meet the next onrushing challenge. We will have to live by faith, trusting God on the very edge – just as the heroes of the faith did, both large and small, who are honored in Hebrews 11.

We may be among the unknowns, but I am convinced that as a generation, we can also be listed among the heroes of faith. So as I close this book I want to tell you about three boomers sure to make the faith hall of fame – faithful people who have given themselves to the task of living by faith, even as they live on the edge.

Valerie the Cross Bearer

Valerie is a boomer in her early fifties. She lives with her husband in a modest house, and they have three children. Valerie has a heart for people and has been a longtime leader in her church, serving in vacation Bible school and ministering to the bereaved at funerals. She always seems to apply just the right touch to make people feel cared for and nurtured.

Valerie is also a child care specialist who teaches at a local community college, training young people to do what she has done so well in the care and nurture of her own children. She is known for being consistently encouraging and enthusiastic as she shepherds her students and colleagues along life's pathway.

A few years ago, Valerie's father died of a heart attack. When she went to comfort her mother, she discovered the truth of what her father had been covering up for years. Her mother had been slipping behind the heavy curtain of Alzheimer's. Her father had hidden it so well—managing the house, cooking all the meals, helping his wife dress, answering questions—that Valerie had no idea just how vulnerable her mother had become.

"I was aware she was losing her memory, but I had no idea she had become so dependent on Dad," Valerie said. The day her father died, Valerie discovered that her mother could not cook a meal for herself, take care of any of her finances, or even make appropriate decisions about dressing herself. After the funeral ended, Valerie had little choice but to load her mother in the car with a few clothes and bring her back home with her, because she certainly couldn't stay by herself.

But Valerie already had an issue at home with regard to her son, Matt. Matt was twenty-two at the time his grandfather died, but he hadn't had much connection with his grandfather. You see, Matt has Down syndrome, and although he functions well in many settings—he went to school and now has a job at a local grocery store—he has occasional behavioral outbursts in which he gets angry and destroys property or becomes sexually aggressive to the point of inappropriateness. Matt can do fine, but he can also do very badly. He needs his mother and father to keep a close eye on him. Matt has always demanded a significant amount of their care and nurture, and now the home also included Valerie's mother, who was becoming increasingly immobilized and baffled by Alzheimer's. Having Valerie's mom in the home confused Matt, and he didn't respond well. He had times each week when he would get angry and jealous of the time she required from his parents. At one point, Matt became so angry that he pounded the bathroom wall hard enough to break several tiles.

And then there was Valerie's mother. During the first few months of living with Valerie's family, she simply seemed confused most of the time. She couldn't quite grasp the reality that her husband had died. She was cooperative when directed by Valerie and could spend time by herself when necessary, but as the disease progressed over the next year, she became more and more disoriented as to time and place. She needed more help with simple hygiene tasks, going to the bathroom, and getting dressed in the morning. Throughout the first year, she had been content just watching television or reading a magazine. But now she was becoming more agitated, always looking for something and then becoming angry because she couldn't find whatever she was trying to locate—something she couldn't even name.

As the disease began closing down her mind, Valerie's mom responded by closing down her world. She became very jealous and protective of Valerie, hovering around her while she was making dinner or getting dressed. Valerie would wake up in the middle of the night to find her mother standing over her, only a few inches from her face. Her mom would become angry and slightly aggressive when Valerie showed the slightest concern about or interest in Matt or her husband. Of course, such behavior aggravated Matt's own jealous tendencies, and so each played off the other, pulling Valerie in opposite directions.

Such constant tugging would have pulled most people apart. But Valerie is a different sort of individual. I never saw her become negative, and she was careful to stay connected to her husband through enjoying short trips and respites together. She kept on working faithfully at her job, and then, as her mother got worse, she had home health aides come to the house for a few hours in the morning and a few in the evening.

Valerie remained vital and encouraging to Matt and his work. She would spend time with him every morning before he would go to work. She also stayed in close contact with his supervisors. Somehow, with everything on her plate, she also managed to keep participating in her women's Bible study, and she always was willing to give a listening ear to a young mother struggling with a challenging child.

I often wondered what kept Valerie going through all the giving. One day I saw her at our local mall, strolling down the walkway, with her mother on one side and Matt on the other. Her mother had her jaw firmly set and a blank stare on her face, yet keeping perfect pace with Valerie's walk. Valerie would turn to her and say simple things such as, "Let's count the steps, Mother," or "You used to take me in that store when I was younger and buy me shoes." Matt's burly frame lumbered along, and Valerie would turn to him every few moments and say something encouraging such as, "Matt, I am so pleased to have you as my son," or "You are the apple of my eye." And in those times when Valerie wasn't saying something directly to her mother or to Matt, she would break into a chorus of "What a Friend We Have in Jesus," her beautiful alto voice brightening the very air itself.

And so there Valerie was, guiding her cognitively impaired

mother with love and care, then spinning her head to the other side to encourage her son to keep working and do his best. These two people, both of whom greatly relied on Valerie, somehow managed to coexist.

Valerie is a boomer hero of the faith. On her course through the mall, she bore all the impairment and problems of two beautiful people who couldn't possibly manage on their own. Just as Jesus bore the burden of the cross on his way to Calvary, Valerie bore the burden of her mother and her son through her patient caregiving. She was willing to give her life so they could have what they needed.

I saw in Valerie that day a woman totally willing to pour herself out for others and to patiently bear the pain and sorrow of their infirmities. I observed no hint of shame in her walk with these infirm folks, only love and giving. Surely she mirrored the attitude of Jesus as he bore our sins on the way to the death on the cross that gained us our redemption.

Doug the Water Walker

Doug, a company manager, heads up the computer team for keeping a local operation online and functioning. He worked hard to have his life in order so that his wife of thirty-five years could stay home to raise their four children. For years, everything about them was defined by stability, steadiness, and predictability.

While they regularly attended church, their service wouldn't have been characterized as either remarkable or up-front. They were givers, supporters, and servers—yet quieter than most members of their age group. Their two oldest children lived solid lives through high school and college before leaving home to pursue careers. They found spouses and got married. As the youngest son closed in on his last two years of college, he looked as stable as his older siblings.

But then there was Don, Doug's third child.

Don began college the same way his older siblings did, with the same type of predictable success. But starting in his second year, he became enticed by a fun-loving crowd. He met his new friends quite innocently at sporting events and would hang out with them in the local bars. Soon he was drinking heavily and hosting drinking parties at his apartment. Don would still go to church, primarily to convince himself that he could drink and be committed to Christ at the same time. But he finally had to admit that he was starting to miss the bottle more at church than he missed Christ when he was drinking.

Don might have slid along for years down a predictable path toward alcoholism and perhaps even drug abuse, but something set Don straight, never to drink again—something horrible. One day, Don was at a friend's house, watching a ball game and doing the requisite drinking. When the game ended, Don hopped in his car, sped onto the expressway—and immediately swerved into an eighteen-wheeler. The truck and trailer jack-knifed in the middle lane and then smashed into a concrete median. Neither Don nor the truck driver was harmed, but a small car on the other side of the truck got slammed into the barrier. The driver, an eighteen-year-old high school senior who was returning home from watching the same game at a friend's house, was impaled in the side in the wreckage of his own car and bled to death before he could receive aid.

Don was arrested and convicted not only of driving under the influence but also of manslaughter, which resulted in six months of jail time and ten years of probation.

"My life seemed to unravel right before my eyes," he said. "The time from when I left my friend's house until I was released from jail seemed like a journey of a million miles. I woke up to find myself in a whole different universe. My friends were totally gone – some didn't want to associate with me ever again, while others just drifted away and moved on with their lives. The boy who got killed was popular in our town, and people looked at me like I was a leper. When you are responsible for someone's death, especially because *you* were irresponsible, people really get angry and feel like you should have been the one to die. I can't really blame them, because not a day has gone by but that I wish it had been me instead of him."

Don lost his grip and went into a deep depression. He slunk back to his father's house, closed the door, and never wanted to surface again.

But Doug was a steady man. Although he always looked unspectacular in his work and in his faith, he was a quiet man of courage, unafraid to go into dangerous places. He stood by Don without question or reservation – a rock of strength and faithfulness. He never excused Don's irresponsibility, but he never budged from remaining totally committed – to coming alongside his son and loving him unconditionally.

"I just kept telling him," Doug said, "that God wasn't through using him and that this was now a part of who he was – it wasn't going to be pleasant to walk through, for sure, but he was going to have a good life."

Doug sat right behind Don at his trial, never failing to maintain association with his son. He was there with Don at every visitation opportunity throughout his imprisonment. Doug kept reminding him about his possibilities and encouraging him not to give in to the sadness and hurt of the past.

But when Don moved back home after his time in jail, Don couldn't fathom how any good could ever come from his life. Doug refused to allow his son to just fade into the background and perhaps slide once again toward alcoholism. He insisted that his son come with him to restaurants and to church – places where he was sure to be seen by others who knew the story. When a woman at church who had been deeply hurt by the death of the boy accused Don of being a murderer, Doug stood right beside his son. After Don apologized to the sobbing woman, Doug said, "Don has said he was sorry, and we do wish we could make things different, but we can't. But Don is my son, and I know he is no murderer. We will have to move on."

Doug's words may not have provided much comfort for the woman, but they did keep driving the point home to Don that he was not alone.

"These kinds of encounters made me just want to fold in on myself and quit, but Dad stood beside me," Don said.

But Doug didn't stop there. He also helped Don by doing what may have been the hardest thing of all—setting some clear boundaries with his son.

"We went slowly at first," Doug explained, "but I told Don that he was an adult and that while his mother and I wanted to help, we just couldn't make life work for him by ourselves."

Doug asked Don for a two-year plan. All along, he kept encouraging Don that even though this tragedy was now a part of his life, his life was far from over. He told Don that if he wanted to continue to receive his father's help, Don needed to devise a plan for his education, employment, and counseling. For each of the three elements of the plan, Doug would supply Don with some resources but would not draw up the plan.

At first, Don didn't respond. "I think it was the depression," Don said, "but I had trouble conceiving how life would go on for me. But then Dad took me to lunch one day and told me that the time had come for me to decide whether to move on or whether I would sink where I was. He told me I had a week to pull together a plan, or I would have to move out on my own. It was a hard reality, but it was also good because it made me face myself again and really decide what I was going to do."

Don did come up with a plan. He started going to counseling and came up with a way not only to finish his undergraduate degree but also to pursue a master's degree in counseling. He began working as a laborer in construction, and after six months, he began giving his parents a little money each month.

Don finally got to the point where he felt the need to meet the parents of the boy who had been killed in the accident. It was a tough decision, but one that Doug supported not only in words but also in action. When the time came to go, Doug was there, right beside his son.

"Dad didn't say anything until we were leaving," Don said, "but he was there with me. It just gave me the confidence that I was not alone, no matter what happened."

What did Don say? He talked about how he would give anything to do the night over and would gladly take the place of the boy. He also asked for forgiveness. He said he had come to understand that the parents couldn't offer complete forgiveness for what he had done to their son and to them, but he wondered if they could find it in their hearts to not wish him harm so he could move on and make his life count for something good.

"I am so sorry," he said through tears, "but I cannot bring your son back, and I have to somehow move on." Doug, at his son's side the whole time, put his hand on Don's back to comfort him.

Doug is a boomer hero of the faith. He could have stayed where he was, in the safety of his life's circumstances as Don stepped into the treacherous waters of pain, prison, and depression. He could have concluded that Don's poor choices and even his tragic consequences were not his responsibility. But Doug stepped out of his well-ordered life and went to Don in the dangerous muck and mire of recovery, reconciliation, and responsibility. He stood by Don when people condemned his son, hurling judgment, anger, and insult at him. When Don sank, he was there, giving every opportunity for Don to take hold.

But Doug did not "save" his son, as tempted as he may have been to do so. Instead, he got out of his boat and offered his hand to his sinking son. Don had to take hold and pull himself out, with his father's help. Just as Jesus offered Peter his hand when the water-walking disciple lost his faith in the middle of wild waves and howling wind (see Matthew 14:22–33), so Doug went to Don to offer his hand — but he waited until Don took the responsibility to take hold. Doug was a water walker, willing to go where it is not safe, so he could help a son in a desperate situation. Doug stayed where the water was rough, helping Don get his life back on track despite enormous odds.

Joanne the Miracle Multiplier

Joanne had enjoyed a great career as an English teacher in the public schools, and she had been able to take an advantageous retirement option at the age of sixty. When her husband died from an aggressive cancer, she anticipated a life of traveling, being involved with friends, and doing all the projects she had put off for years. She never anticipated that her strong, vigorous, and mentally sharp mother would one day need so much help.

Joanne's mother fell and broke her hip and needed not only care but constant encouragement to rehabilitate. At first, Joanne accompanied her mother to the rehabilitation center where she had gone right after surgery; after her mom's discharge, Joanne visited her at her home four or five times a day. As Joanne worked with her mother, she began to realize that all the skills she had utilized when her husband was dying of cancer — encouragement, scheduling, and nurture — were easily transferable to the realities of caring for her mother.

"I knew how the health care system worked," she said. "I knew how the process of letting go worked; I knew how to organize information to get the needed services; and I knew how to say good-bye at the end and get through the pain and grief of death. Just because the experience of a broken hip was different and the organizations were different, it didn't mean I couldn't use my skills in this new situation."

Before long, Joanne had decided to sell her home and move into her mother's house. She not only helped her mother rehabilitate but also taught her how to organize her life and take better care of herself. Joanne's mother recovered and soon was functioning more as a companion to her daughter than as someone in need of care. Joanne had drifted from her church after her husband had died, and many of the old "couple friendships" she once shared there had ended. So she decided to go with her mom to her mom's church for a time.

"What I saw when I walked in was salt-and-pepper – large empty spaces in the dark-stained pews, sprinkled with a few bodies, all of whom had white hair." To all appearances, this small Methodist church was dying off.

Joanne met the minister, and they talked for a while. She was impressed with how familiar he was with her mother and how he had noted her new vitality and progress. "Most older people in this church start the long slide toward final decline after breaking a hip," he said, "but your mother has come back stronger than ever." He inquired about what had made the difference, and Joanne explained how she had been privileged to come alongside her mom and help her during her time of need.

"I have so many in my congregation who are facing the same problems," he said. "I wonder if you would be willing to help them." Joanne agreed – thinking she'd be lucky to get more than one call over the next six months.

She was very wrong.

By the middle of the following week, Joanne had received three phone calls from the minister, inquiring about three different parishioners who were on the pathway to needing caregiving. Joanne and her mother went to visit all three of them.

"We sort of developed a rhythm of teamwork," Joanne said. "I did the things I do in terms of giving them a simplified way of keeping things straight financially, organizing their homes so they can stay in them, helping them manage and keep their medications up-to-date, and sharing the simple things they can do to maintain their own nutrition. But my mom was the real encourager. She would get in there and say, 'You need to listen to my daughter. I know these things work because they worked for me. You can make these simple changes, and things *will* get better for you."

One elderly individual ended up needing full-time assistance, but for six weeks Joanne and her mother visited the other two for a couple of hours each week. They would go over the same types of changes, integrate a few new ones, and encourage their new friends. In two months, the two elderly people had improved significantly. One day, the daughter of one of them contacted Joanne.

"I've been trying to get my mother to make some of these changes for over a year," she said, "and you and your mother got her to do it in a month. I can't thank you enough."

Joanne soon discovered she had a knack for quasi-social work, training, and organizing, while her mother had a real gift for encouraging and teaching how to implement changes. They were a team, and together they made a big difference in two people's lives.

That's when the wheels in Joanne's brain *really* started turning. She was a master at managing her own retirement resources and realized the time might come when she would have to return to work, but always assumed it would have something to do with substitute teaching. But now she saw an opportunity. She and her mother discussed the idea and agreed on the plan.

Joanne took the money from the sale of her house and dedicated it to a new ministry of helping older people make the changes that would allow them to stay in their homes. After he saw the positive changes in the lives of Joanne's mother and the two other parishioners, the minister offered to support Joanne's idea and encouraged her to work out of an office in the church.

Joanne and her mother were soon evaluating and encouraging five members of the congregation and helping them get situated for the long haul of aging. Then they turned their attention to the parishioners who were no longer able to attend worship. In each case, Joanne and her mother dedicated two hours a week for six weeks to help the older person get organized, make changes, and receive encouragement and practical tips from Joanne's mother. Although more than half of those they worked with needed more care, Joanne helped them access services and helped their families figure out how to best get the assistance they needed. Joanne and her mother used the money they had dedicated for this ministry to buy simple things that would help the folks get organized; and every now and then, they used some of the money to help the older people financially. It was turning out to be quite a ministry!

"Over the course of a year, I still saw salt-and-pepper when I walked into the church, but there was definitely more salt scattered throughout the room," Joanne said. Because of Joanne's efforts, first with her mom and then with her mom's congregation, about one-third of the people they worked with began returning to church.

But it didn't stop there. Joanne and her mother started a Sunday morning class, taught in eight-week intervals, that was designed for older people and caregivers. Joanne showed them her organizing and simplifying tips, while her mother added her own unique contribution. As word got around, another church contacted Joanne and her mother about coming to teach the class to that congregation. Slowly and surely, they began to have ten to twenty older people and caregivers show up for their classes, and the referrals from the minister and his colleagues began to grow.

This isn't a miracle story of church growth, even though Joanne's mom's church soon stabilized its membership and even started nudging upward. But the ministry that Joanne and her mother started—now that's another story. It began a miraculous growth.

"When we would go to someone's house or when we'd meet in our Sunday class, people would offer to pay me something," Joanne said. "I would just suggest they could make a donation to the ministry." Surprisingly, people who had received help did just that, and by the end of one year, the money she had originally donated had actually *grown*. Two years after Joanne had first set foot in her mother's church, the fund for the support of this ministry had doubled.

At that time, the minister came to Joanne and her mother and asked if they would be willing to be part-time employees of the church, doing exactly what they had been doing so effectively as volunteers. At ages sixty-two and eighty-two, Joanne and her mother began successful part-time careers helping older people better manage their lives and encouraging them to make necessary changes so they could live more active lives. They received part-time salaries, and the ministry continues to grow to this day.

Joanne is a boomer hero. She took what she had in the way of skills and knowledge and turned it into service. When her mother responded positively, they took their meager beginning and turned it into something that greatly blessed others. Just as Jesus took a few fish and loaves from a small boy and turned them into a meal that satisfied a huge, hungry crowd (see John 6:1–13), so Joanne and her mother saw the joyful results of multiplying what they were willing to give.

Joanne is an effective caregiver who went a step beyond to find the place where her talents and skills could multiply the talents and skills of others. The money she gave turned into more and more money—resources that are now being used to pay her a salary for a new and unexpected career. She is a multiplier of miracles to the people she serves.

We Are One with Jesus

As a group, we boomers are good people. We are people of change and of challenge. We adjust, adapt, and acclimate to the world, maybe like no other generation before us. We have been seen as self-centered and irresponsible, particularly by our predecessors in the Greatest Generation. But as the three examples in this chapter illustrate, I believe we are enormously caring, extraordinarily loyal, and endlessly resourceful.

We are the boomers, and we are the Caregiving Generation.

We are the generation that will change the first part of this century by the way we care for our elders and for our adult children who have difficulty adjusting to life, as well as by the way we adapt and care for ourselves with limited retirement resources. It will not be an easy life. In many cases, it will not be a happy life. But it will be a life in which we fulfill not only a purpose of care but also a purpose of identity—the identity of Jesus Christ, who lived a life of service.

The stories of Valerie, Doug, and Joanne remind me so much of a passage of Scripture that isn't talked about much in our churches or Bible studies. It was a hard saying of Jesus when he first spoke it, and it is a hard saying now:

> "I tell you the truth, he who believes has everlasting life.
> I am the bread of life. Your forefathers ate the manna in the
> desert, yet they died. But here is the bread that comes down

from heaven, which a man may eat and not die. I am living bread that came down from heaven. If anyone eats of this bread, he will live forever. This bread is my flesh, which I will give for the life of the world."

John 6:47–51

The statement disturbed the Jews, and they began to grumble about Jesus calling himself the bread of heaven and telling them that they must eat his flesh.

Jesus did not back down. In fact, he went much further:

"I tell you the truth, unless you eat the flesh of the Son of Man and drink his blood, you have no life in you. Whoever eats my flesh and drinks my blood has eternal life, and I will raise him up at the last day. For my flesh is real food and my blood is real drink. Whoever eats my flesh and drinks my blood remains in me, and I in him."

John 6:53–56

Wow! Imagine how the Jews who heard Jesus felt about these unsettling words. Imagine how it feels to *us* when we hear Jesus call us to do the same – all this flesh eating and blood drinking. It sounds not only radical but gross!

But Jesus said it just as he meant it. He calls us to come to him. He calls us to consume his body and his blood and integrate who he is into us. He sets the Holy Spirit in us as the mark that he is in us. And with Jesus, we gain wonderful access into who he is and what he has done for each of us. He becomes a part of us, taking on our sins and ministering in our darkest places. He compensates for who we are by matching his sacrificial perfection with our imperfections and working out reconciliation with God and forgiveness for our sins. He commends to us his power, grace, and sanctifying beauty into a perfection we can use for our joyful entrance into the kingdom of God. He is who we are, and he makes us eternally his through the gift of life everlasting.

But make no mistake about it—to gain access to everything Jesus wants for us, we must consume him into our hearts, just as surely as if we ate his body and drank his blood. His substance has to be part of us in spirit and in truth. If we are to be a part of Jesus, then it is likely—even inevitable—that we will feel part of his struggle and pain that moves humanity toward redemption. As the apostle Paul declared, "It has been granted to you on behalf of Christ not only to believe on him, but also to suffer for him, since you are going through the same struggle you saw I had, and now hear that I still have" (Philippians 1:29–30).

The knife definitely cuts both ways. Jesus will become part of us, and we will become part of him. When we become one with Jesus, his heart starts beating in our hearts; his concern starts becoming our concern; his pain starts becoming our pain. When Christ becomes a part of us, we also become a part of him. And we will start finding ourselves following his Spirit into the dark places of sin and pain; we will seek out neediness and poverty; we will seek out those who are in need of a Savior.

Of course, that kingdom Savior is Jesus himself, but often, that Savior is embodied in us. In spirit and in truth, we are the body of Christ. He is in us, and we are in him—and we will follow him where his heart goes. We will go to the darkest places of sin, to the most tragic and hopeless cases of need, to the hardest places of accusation and misunderstanding. This is where we will stand and where we will serve, because this is the place that Christ serves.

Boomers are the Caregiving Generation, first and foremost, because Jesus is the great caregiver. He has no hesitation to clean up the awful messes our parents make when they lose control of their bowels or vomit up what they cannot keep down. He has no problem dealing with the stench of death that breathes its putrid residue into our nostrils as our parents decay and decline before our very eyes. He has no difficulty seeing and executing the practical things that need to be done in terms of care, nurture, and organization with our parents, even though the demand is great.

He will go to the place of training and understanding with our adult children. He has a heart of patience and understanding as he encourages them to learn new skills amid the harsh realities of learning how to "do life." He has the strength and stamina to help and the wisdom to know when to demand that our adult children help themselves.

And he has no fear as he looks into our future, when we may well have more need than resources to meet the need. He is absolutely faithful in giving and serving, whether we have plenty or whether we are in want, because he will somehow make the resources work.

Jesus cares and is capable. And because we are in him, we also care and will be capable. We have eaten his body and drunk his blood. We bring Jesus to this world that so urgently needs his care. We bear his wounds and his cross of caregiving, because we are one with Jesus.

It is no mistake that Jesus used the metaphor of bread to signify his body and wine his blood. When we participate in Communion, Jesus doesn't want us to remember only his sacrifice and his atonement for our sins; he also wants us to remember that we indeed are inextricably tied to him.

Everywhere we go as caregiving boomers, he goes also. Everywhere he goes as a seeker of the lost, a minister to the needy, and a caregiver of humanity, we also go. We are in him, and he is in us. Communion reminds us that we are bound together with Jesus in the task of caregiving for the sake of the kingdom, and that as we give care, we will be changed to live and love like Jesus.

Boomers are on the edge. We are on the edge of the great challenge of learning how to care for our parents, of instructing our adult children about how to move toward independence, and of planning for resourceful and anxiety-free living in a world where we will have less. But I truly believe our generation is here for a reason. We are here because *Jesus is here.* His heart is right here, and it is caught up with the needs and concerns of our parents, our adult children, and us as we think about our scarcity of resources. We are not alone.

So let us step off the edge into the arms of Jesus. Let us serve with his heart and his will. That is how we will make all the difference in the world.

Loving Your Parents When They Can No Longer Love You

Terry Hargrave

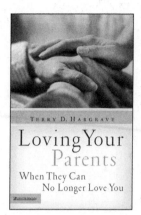

- Insights on caring for an aging parent
- Timely guidance for the challenges
- Encouragement for the journey

You had plans for this time in your life, but now a parent needs care. It's a confusing, stressful, and exhausting time. But it can also be a time of remarkable spiritual growth. *Loving Your Parents When They Can No Longer Love You* helps you navigate your role as caregiver with God's grace and guidance. And it alerts you to the difficult issues you may face, such as:

- Legal and financial decisions
- How much care will be needed and when
- Evaluating different living options
- Depression, dementia, and Alzheimer's disease
- Caring for a parent who has mistreated you
- Accepting and planning for death

Most important, this book helps you embrace caregiving as a spiritual journey that will deepen your faith and strengthen your character. It not only opens your eyes to the realities of caregiving; it also teaches you how to allow God to change your life for the better.

Softcover 978-0-310-25563-5

Pick up a copy today at your favorite bookstore!

Strength and Courage for Caregivers

30 Hope-Filled Morning and Evening Reflections

Terry Hargrave

Support, respite, and encouragement for those who care for others

Taking care of a family member who is ill, disabled, or dying requires courage, strength, commitment, and love. Now Terry Hargrave, an expert in counseling and caregiving, offers you help with a devotional written with your specific needs in mind. The morning prayers and evening reflections in this book are short and to the point. *Strength and Courage for Caregivers* weaves together powerful stories, practical advice, and the restorative promises of Scripture, reminding caregivers that they are not alone in this important yet all too often unacknowledged and underappreciated work.

Hardcover, Jacketed 978-0-310-27769-9

Pick up a copy today at your favorite bookstore!

Share Your Thoughts

With the Author: Your comments will be forwarded to
the author when you send them to *zauthor@zondervan.com*.

With Zondervan: Submit your review of this book
by writing to *zreview@zondervan.com*.

Free Online Resources at
www.zondervan.com/hello

 Zondervan AuthorTracker: Be notified whenever your
favorite authors publish new books, go on tour, or post
an update about what's happening in their lives.

 Daily Bible Verses and Devotions: Enrich your life
with daily Bible verses or devotions that help you start
every morning focused on God.

 Free Email Publications: Sign up for newsletters on
fiction, Christian living, church ministry, parenting, and
more.

 Zondervan Bible Search: Find and compare
Bible passages in a variety of translations at
www.zondervanbiblesearch.com.

 Other Benefits: Register yourself to receive online
benefits like coupons and special offers, or to participate
in research.